ASIAN POLITICAL, ECONOMIC AND SECURITY ISSUES

BANGLADESH AND BURMA: BACKGROUND AND ISSUES

ASIAN POLITICAL, ECONOMIC AND SECURITY ISSUES

Additional books in this series can be found on Nova's website under the Series tab.

Additional E-books in this series can be found on Nova's website under the E-books tab.

FOREIGN POLICY OF THE UNITED STATES

Additional books in this series can be found on Nova's website under the Series tab.

Additional E-books in this series can be found on Nova's website under the E-books tab.

ASIAN POLITICAL, ECONOMIC AND SECURITY ISSUES

BANGLADESH AND BURMA: BACKGROUND AND ISSUES

BRANDON E. STROMBERG
EDITOR

Nova Science Publishers, Inc.
New York

Copyright © 2011 by Nova Science Publishers, Inc.

All rights reserved. No part of this book may be reproduced, stored in a retrieval system or transmitted in any form or by any means: electronic, electrostatic, magnetic, tape, mechanical photocopying, recording or otherwise without the written permission of the Publisher.

For permission to use material from this book please contact us:
Telephone 631-231-7269; Fax 631-231-8175
Web Site: http://www.novapublishers.com

NOTICE TO THE READER
The Publisher has taken reasonable care in the preparation of this book, but makes no expressed or implied warranty of any kind and assumes no responsibility for any errors or omissions. No liability is assumed for incidental or consequential damages in connection with or arising out of information contained in this book. The Publisher shall not be liable for any special, consequential, or exemplary damages resulting, in whole or in part, from the readers' use of, or reliance upon, this material. Any parts of this book based on government reports are so indicated and copyright is claimed for those parts to the extent applicable to compilations of such works.

Independent verification should be sought for any data, advice or recommendations contained in this book. In addition, no responsibility is assumed by the publisher for any injury and/or damage to persons or property arising from any methods, products, instructions, ideas or otherwise contained in this publication.

This publication is designed to provide accurate and authoritative information with regard to the subject matter covered herein. It is sold with the clear understanding that the Publisher is not engaged in rendering legal or any other professional services. If legal or any other expert assistance is required, the services of a competent person should be sought. FROM A DECLARATION OF PARTICIPANTS JOINTLY ADOPTED BY A COMMITTEE OF THE AMERICAN BAR ASSOCIATION AND A COMMITTEE OF PUBLISHERS.

Additional color graphics may be available in the e-book version of this book.

LIBRARY OF CONGRESS CATALOGING-IN-PUBLICATION DATA

Bangladesh and Burma : background and issues / editor, Brandon E. Stromberg.
 p. cm.
 Includes index.
 ISBN 978-1-61761-219-0 (hardcover)
 1. United States--Foreign relations--Bangladesh. 2. Bangladesh--Foreign relations--United States. 3. United States--Foreign relations--Burma. 4. Burma--Foreign relations--United States. 5. Bangladesh--Politics and government--1971- 6. Burma--Politics and government--1988- I. Stromberg, Brandon E.
 JZ1480.A57B3 2010
 327.7305492--dc22
                           2010031172

Published by Nova Science Publishers, Inc. ✦ New York

CONTENTS

Preface   vii

Chapter 1   Bangladesh: Political and Strategic Developments and United States Interests   1
Bruce Vaughn

Chapter 2   Bangladesh: Background and United States Relations   29
Bruce Vaughn

Chapter 3   Burma's 2010 Elections: Implications of the New Constitution and Election Law   51
Michael F. Martin

Chapter 4   Burma and Transnational Crime   79
Liana Sun Wyler

Chapter 5   Burma: Economic Sanctions   99
Larry A. Niksch and Martin A. Weiss

Chapter 6   Statement of Senator Richard G. Lugar, East Asian and Pacific Affairs Subcommittee of the Foreign Relations Committee   107
Richard G. Lugar

Chapter 7   Testimony of Kurt Campbell, Assistant Secretary of State, Bureau of East Asian and Pacific Affairs, before the Subcommittee on East Asian and Pacific Affairs, Hearing on "U.S. Policy toward Burma"   109

Contents

Chapter 8	Testimony of Dr. Thant Myint-U, before the East Asia Sub-Committee of the Senate Foreign Relations Committee	**115**
Chapter 9	Testimony of David I. Steinberg, Professor, School of Foreign Service, Georgetown University, before the United States Senate Subcommittee on Asia and Pacific Affairs, Hearings on Burma	**125**
Chapter 10	Testimony of David C. Williams, Executive Director, Center for Consitutional Democracy, John S. Hastings Professor of Law, Indiana University Maurer School of Law, before the Senate Foreign Relations Subcommittee on East Asia and Pacific Affairs, Hearing on "U.S. Policy toward Burma: Its Impact and Effectiveness"	**139**
Chapter Sources		**147**
Index		**149**

PREFACE

This book explores the historical background and political and strategic developments in both Bangladesh and Burma. Bangladesh is a densely populated and poor nation in South Asia. Roughly 80% of its population lives on less than $2 a day. Bangladesh suffers from high levels of corruption and an at times faltering democratic system that have been subject to pressure from the military. Transnational organized crime groups in Burma (Myanmar) operate a multi-billion dollar criminal industry that stretches across Southeast Asia . Trafficked drugs, humans, wildlife, gems, timber, and other contraband flow through Burma, supporting the illicit demands of the region and beyond. Transnational crime in Burma bears upon U.S. interests as it threatens regional security in Southeast Asia and bolsters a regime that fosters a culture of corruption and disrespect for the rule of law and human rights.

Chapter 1- Bangladesh is a densely populated and poor nation in South Asia. Roughly 80% of its population lives on less than $2 a day. Its population is largely Muslim and its geography is dominated by its low-lying riparian aspect. Bangladesh suffers from high levels of corruption and an at times faltering democratic system that has been subject to pressure from the military.

Bangladesh (the former East Pakistan) gained its independence in 1971, following India's intervention in a rebellion against West Pakistan (currently called Pakistan). In the years since independence, Bangladesh has established a reputation as a largely moderate and democratic majority Muslim country. This status has been under threat from a combination of political violence, weak governance, poverty, corruption, and Islamist militancy. There has been concern in the past that should Bangladesh become a failed state, or a state with increased influence by Islamist extremists, it could serve as a base of operations for terrorist activity. In more recent years, such concerns have abated somewhat as Islamist militants have been vigorously pursued by the government and Bangladesh has returned to democratic government.

Chapter 2- Bangladesh (the former East Pakistan) gained its independence in 1971, following India's intervention in a rebellion against West Pakistan (currently called Pakistan). Democratic elections in 1991 ended two decades of authoritarian rule in Dhaka. The Bangladesh National Party (BNP), which led the ruling coalition of the previous government, and the leading opposition party, the Awami League (AL), traditionally have dominated Bangladeshi politics. The BNP is led by former Prime Minister Khaleda Zia while the AL is led by Sheikh Hasina. Bangladesh has been a largely moderate and democratic majority Muslim country. This status has been under threat from a combination of political violence, weak governance, poverty, corruption, and Islamist militancy. When in opposition, both parties have sought to regain control of the government through demonstrations, labor strikes, and transport blockades.

Chapter 3- On an undisclosed date in 2010, Burma plans to hold its first parliamentary elections in 20 years. The elections are to be held under a new constitution, supposedly approved in a national referendum held in 2008 in the immediate aftermath of the widespread destruction caused by Cyclone Nargis. The official results of the constitutional referendum are widely seen as fraudulent, but despite significant domestic and international opposition, Burma's ruling military junta—the State Peace and Development Council (SPDC)—has insisted on conducting the polls as part of what it calls a path to "disciplined democracy."

On March 9, 2010, the SPDC released five new laws for the pending parliamentary elections. Three of the laws are about the three main types of parliaments stipulated in the constitution—the two houses of the national parliament (*Pyidaungsu Hluttaw*) and the Regional or State parliaments. The fourth law—the Political Parties Registration Law—sets conditions for the registration and operation of political parties in Burma; the fifth law establishes a Union Election Commission to supervise the parliamentary elections and political parties.

Chapter 4- Transnational organized crime groups in Burma (Myanmar) operate a multi-billion dollar criminal industry that stretches across Southeast Asia. Trafficked drugs, humans, wildlife, gems, timber, and other contraband flow through Burma, supporting the illicit demands of the region and beyond. Widespread collusion between traffickers and Burma's ruling military junta, the State Peace and Development Council (SPDC), allows organized crime groups to function with impunity. Transnational crime in Burma bears upon U.S. interests as it threatens regional security in Southeast Asia and bolsters a regime that fosters a culture of corruption and disrespect for the rule of law and human rights.

Chapter 5- On October 19, 2007, President George W. Bush issued Executive Order 13449. This followed a September 25, 2007 statement by President Bush that sanctions against Burma, which have been in place since 1997, would be tightened to specifically target leading Burmese officials and impose additional financial and travel sanctions. This chapter provides background information on existing economic sanctions against Burma and possible options to expand sanctions.

Chapter 6 – This is a statement of Senator Richard G. Lugar, East Asian and Pacific Affairs Subcommittee of the Foreign Relations Committee, before the East Asian and Pacific Affairs Subcommittee of the Foreign Relations Committee.

Chapter 7 – This is a statement of Kurt Campbell, Assistant Secretary of State, Bureau of East Asian and Pacific Affairs, United States Department of State, before the Subcommittee on east Asian and Pcific Affairs Senate Foreign Relations Committee.

Chapter 8 – This is a statement of Doctor Thant Myint-U, before the East Asia Subcomittee of the Senate Foreign Relations Committee.

Chapter 9 – This is a statement of David I. Steinberg, Professor, School of Foreign Service, Georgetown University, before the United Senate Subcommittee on Asia and Pacific Affairs

Chapter 10 – This is a statement of David C. Williams, Executive Director, Center for Constitutional Democracy, John S. Hastings Professor of Law, Indiana University Maurer School of Law, before the Senate Committee on Foreign Relations Subcommittee on East Asia and Pacific Affiars.

In: Bangladesh and Burma: Background and Issues ISBN: 978-1-61761-219-0
Editor: Brandon E. Stromberg © 2011 Nova Science Publishers, Inc.

Chapter 1

BANGLADESH: POLITICAL AND STRATEGIC DEVELOPMENTS AND UNITED STATES INTERESTS

Bruce Vaughn

SUMMARY

Bangladesh is a densely populated and poor nation in South Asia. Roughly 80% of its population lives on less than $2 a day. Its population is largely Muslim and its geography is dominated by its low-lying riparian aspect. Bangladesh suffers from high levels of corruption and an at times faltering democratic system that has been subject to pressure from the military.

Bangladesh (the former East Pakistan) gained its independence in 1971, following India's intervention in a rebellion against West Pakistan (currently called Pakistan). In the years since independence, Bangladesh has established a reputation as a largely moderate and democratic majority Muslim country. This status has been under threat from a combination of political violence, weak governance, poverty, corruption, and Islamist militancy. There has been concern in the past that should Bangladesh become a failed state, or a state with increased influence by Islamist extremists, it could serve as a base of operations for terrorist activity. In more recent years, such concerns have abated somewhat as Islamist militants have been vigorously pursued by the government and Bangladesh has returned to democratic government.

The Bangladesh National Party (BNP) and the Awami League (AL) traditionally have dominated Bangladeshi politics, with the AL in government since January 2009. The BNP is led by former Prime Minister Khaleda Zia; the AL is led by current Prime Minister Sheikh Hasina. When in opposition, both parties have sought to regain control of the government through demonstrations, labor strikes, and transport blockades. Political violence has long been part of the political landscape in Bangladesh. In 2004-2005, a particularly intensive set of bombings raised questions about political stability in the country.

Bangladesh was ruled by a military-backed caretaker government led by Fakhruddin Ahmed for approximately two years prior to the return to democracy that was ushered in by the December 2008 election. The military-backed caretaker government sought to pursue an anti-corruption drive that challenged the usual political elites. It also sought to put in place voter reforms, including issuing identity cards, and moved against militant Islamists.

The current Hasina government came to power in free and fair elections with an overwhelming majority in parliament. It has moved forward with a war crimes tribunal to prosecute atrocities from the 1971 war of independence from Pakistan. The Hasina government has also moved to strengthen ties with both India and China. With the help of the army it successfully suppressed a mutiny by the Bangladesh Rifles in February 2009.

Demographic pressure and environmental problems, some believed to be brought on by climate change, are increasingly a problem for Bangladesh. A rising population when combined with poor economic resilience and limits on the extent to which agricultural output can be expanded could prove to be politically destabilizing in the future.

U.S. policy toward Bangladesh emphasizes support for political stability and democracy, development, and human rights. The United States has long-standing supportive relations with Bangladesh and views Bangladesh as a moderate voice in the Islamic world. The U.S. offers considerable economic assistance to Bangladesh, and has substantial military-to-military ties that include cooperation in multilateral peacekeeping.

OVERVIEW

American Interests in Bangladesh

Bangladesh's moderate Muslim voice and developing democracy means that it is generally well perceived by Washington. American interests with Bangladesh include promoting development, trade, and energy; democracy support; countering militant Islamists; and working together in peace operations. Bangladesh is also of interest to the United States for the role it plays in the larger geopolitical dynamics of South Asia.

United States humanitarian assistance and development support to Bangladesh includes a focus on "stabilizing population growth, protecting human health, encouraging broad-based economic growth, and building democracy."[1] American foreign assistance to Bangladesh in FY2010 is estimated to total $168.5 million. Specific aspects of U.S. foreign assistance are discussed in greater detail below.

American support for developing democracy in Bangladesh has taken on renewed importance with the return of democratic government. American foreign assistance for governing justly and democratically goes to rule of law and human rights, good governance, political competition and consensus building, and civil society programs. Chairman David Price of the House Democracy Partnership led a congressional delegation to Bangladesh in March 2010 to work with Bangladesh to help it strengthen its democratic institutions and processes. The delegation called on the government to work inclusively with opposition parties and for the opposition to work constructively within the legal framework.[2]

Bangladesh-U.S. trade has been expanding in recent years, and the United States is Bangladesh's largest trading partner. Bilateral trade grew from $1 billion in 1992 to $4 billion in 2009. Although the two nations have discussed a Trade and Investment Framework Agreement (TIFA), Bangladeshi concerns over environmental, labor, and intellectual property provisions have made Bangladesh reluctant to move forward with a TIFA. Bangladesh announced in March 2010 that it would welcome any proposed alternative. U.S. Ambassador James Moriarty has indicated that an alternative could be a U.S.-Bangladesh Economic and Trade Cooperation Forum.[3] American trade and investment interests in Bangladesh include developing natural gas reserves thought to be found in the Bay of Bengal off Bangladesh's coast.

Due to the moderate form of Islamic belief that is prevalent in Bangladesh, the country is valued for its "strong secular and democratic heritage" and is a key state in Asia where the United States can try to engage the Muslim world in its struggle against militant Islamists.[4] Bangladesh and the United States have a common interest in working to counter extremist Islamists and their ideology.

Bangladesh is a very active participant in international peace operations. At the beginning of 2010 it was the second-largest contributor of military and police contingents to United Nations Peace Operations with 10,427 personnel involved in such operations.[5]

Bangladesh is situated at the northern extreme of the Bay of Bengal and could potentially be a state of increasing interest in the evolving strategic dynamics between India and China. This importance could be accentuated by the development of Bangladesh's energy reserves and by regional energy and trade routes to China and India.

Key Political Actors in Bangladesh

The complexities of the Bangladesh political landscape can be simplified by identifying its key actors, their institutional and political affiliations, and their interrelationships. In this context, there are four key institutional and individual actors that largely define the Bangladesh political landscape in 2010. These are (1) Prime Minister Sheikh Hasina of the Awami League (AL); (2) Khaleda Zia of the Bangladesh National Party (BNP), which is the key opposition party; (3) Islamist political parties and extremists; and (4) the military.

For much of its history Bangladesh has been ruled by either Hasina or Zia. Both have to varying degrees sought to obstruct the other while in opposition. The intense and at times violent political rivalry between the BNP and the AL, and the presence of radical Islamist parties and groups, have defined Bangladesh's political environment in recent years. The role of the military is another critical element. Bangladesh has only recently emerged from a period of military-backed government that began following convulsive political violence in 2004-2005. There was also a mutiny of members of the Bangladesh Rifles (BDR) that was suppressed by the regular army in 2009.

CONTEMPORARY POLITICAL SITUATION

In 2009, Bangladesh emerged from a period of rule by a military-backed caretaker government through a December 29, 2008, election that gave Prime Minister Sheikh Hasina of the Awami League (AL) a very strong electoral mandate. The AL government is expected to serve its full term, as it has 230 of 299 seats in parliament. Due to its strong victory, the AL has the necessary two-thirds majority needed to amend the constitution and is able to rule without coalition partners.

The elections were considered to be free and fair and led to the peaceful handover of power by the military-backed government of Fakhruddin Ahmed that had ruled for approximately two years.[6] The current leader of the opposition Bangladesh National Party (BNP), Khaleda Zia, was prime minister until she stepped down in October 2006. The prime minister is normally supposed to step down and transfer power to a caretaker government for a short time period immediately preceding elections. Political violence in the lead-up to the scheduled January 2007 election led the caretaker government to declare a state of emergency and extend its rule until the December 2008 elections were held.

Other challenges facing Bangladesh include rampant corruption, dysfunctional parliamentary government, a weak judiciary, a poor human rights record, communal conflict, periodic environmental disasters, and poverty.[7] An estimated 80% of Bangladeshis live on less than two dollars a day.[8] In March 2010, the High Court declared illegal corruption charges that were brought against Prime Minister Hasina during the last BNP-led government.[9]

Despite these challenges, Bangladesh has established a reputation as a largely moderate and democratic majority Muslim country. This status has, however, been under threat. When in opposition, both parties have sought to regain control of the government through demonstrations, labor strikes, and transport blockades. The BNP likely will increasingly use such tactics, as it lacks sufficient representation in parliament at present to mount any substantial opposition to the government in that body. This makes continued control of the military a key aspect of stability for the AL in order to maintain control of the streets.

HISTORICAL BACKGROUND AND GEOGRAPHY

Historical Background

Formerly known as East Pakistan, and before that as the East Bengal region of British India, Bangladesh gained its independence from Pakistan in 1971 following a civil war that included military intervention by India. Whereas the partition of British India into India and Pakistan was the result of religious division between Hindus and Muslims, the partition of Pakistan that created Bangladesh was more the result of ethnic division and the desire for self-expression by Bengalis from East Pakistan. This double partition was a challenge to the rationale for Pakistan and points to the national component of Bengali identity rather than to the religious component that has played an increasingly important role in Bangladesh politics and identity in recent years.[10]

Bangladeshi politics have been characterized by a bitter struggle between the Bangladesh National Party (BNP) and the Awami League (AL), and particularly between the two leaders of the respective parties, former Prime Minister Khaleda Zia (1991-1996, 2001-2006) and Prime Minister Sheikh Hasina Wajed (1996-2001, 2009 to the present). Zia is the widow of former president and military strongman Ziaur Rahman, who was assassinated in 1981. Sheikh Hasina is the daughter of Bangladeshi independence leader and first Prime Minister Sheikh Mujibur Rahman, who was assassinated in 1975. When out of power, both the AL and the BNP have devoted their energies to parliamentary boycotts, demonstrations, and strikes in an effort to unseat the ruling party. The strikes often succeeded in immobilizing the government and disrupting economic activity. The president's powers are largely ceremonial but are expanded during the tenure of a caretaker government.

There has been much political violence in Bangladesh. The State Department issued a statement that "strongly condemned" the bomb attack that killed four, including former Awami League Finance Minister A.M.S. Kibria, and injured 70 at a political rally of the Awami League on January 27, 2005. The incident was described by the State Department as "the latest in a series of often deadly attacks on prominent leaders of the political opposition and civil society." On August 21, 2004, grenades were hurled in an apparent political assassination attempt on opposition leader Sheikh Hasina at a political rally in Dhaka, killing 23. These two attacks, and widespread bombings on August 17, 2005, marked a rising tide of political violence in Bangladesh. The Awami

League has alleged that the Islamist Jamaat-e-Islami and Islamiya Okiyya Jote parties protected the radicals responsible for the violence from prosecution by the government.[11] There was relatively less violence during the period of the military-backed caretaker government.

Geography

Bangladesh is a low-lying riparian nation of much agricultural fertility with a subtropical monsoonal climate that is particularly prone to flooding. The country's alluvial plain is drained by five major river systems that flow into the Bay of Bengal. Approximately 40% of Bangladesh's total land area is flooded each year.[12] It has a large delta at the confluence of the Ganges, Brahmaputra, and Meghana rivers and their tributaries. The southwest coastal jungle region is known as the Sundarbans and is home to some of the few remaining Bengal Tigers in the world. There are some hills in the Chittagong Hill Tract region in the southeast and near Sylhet in the northeast of the country. Bangladesh is subject to major cyclones that cause extensive flooding at the rate of some 16 major floods per decade.[13] The low-lying aspect of Bangladesh's terrain makes it particularly vulnerable to sea-level rise due to climate change.

BANGLADESH IN BRIEF

Population: 156 million; growth rate: 1.29% urban population 27%, urbanization: 3.5% annual rate of change
Land Area: 147,570 sq. km. (slightly smaller than Iowa), 55.39% of which is arable land
Capital: Dhaka, population approx. 10 million
Language: Bengali (official); English widely used
Literacy: 47.9%
Ethnic Groups: Approximately 98% Bengali with some tribal and non-Bengali groups
Religion: Muslim 83%; Hindu 16%
Life Expectancy at Birth: total 60.25 years, male 57.57, female 63.03
Infant Mortality: 59.02 per 1,000 births
Inflation: 7.2%
Poverty: 36.3% are below the poverty line

> **Gross Domestic Product:** 5.7% growth 2010 est. with per capita ppp = $1,600
> **GDP by Sector:** Agriculture 18.7%, industry 28.7%, services 52.6%
> **Labor Force:** Agriculture 45%, industry 30%, services 25%
> **Key Exports:** Garments, frozen fish and seafood, jute, leather
> **Key Export Partners:** U.S. 24%, Germany 15.3%, U.K. 10%, France 7.4%
>
> Sources: CIA, *The World Factbook*; Reuters; BBC News; The Economist Intelligence Unit; U.S. Departments of State and Commerce; World Bank.

GOVERNMENT, ELECTIONS, AND BANGLADESH POLITICS

Government and Elections

An understanding of the traditional close political balance between the two main factions in previous elections provides context to assess the future political landscape in Bangladesh. The January 2007 elections were postponed by the military-backed interim government ostensibly to forestall mounting political violence and remove corrupt officials from office. After two years, the military-backed caretaker government returned Bangladesh to democratically elected government. The Awami League won an overwhelming victory in the December 2008 election, capturing 230 of 299 seats. The Bangladesh unicameral national parliament is known as the Jatiya Sangsad. The number of seats won by the AL does not fully reflect what was really a more closely balanced performance between the two main political factions in Bangladesh, as opposition parties received 40% of the vote in 2008.

During the election held on October 1, 2001, the Zia-led Bangladesh National Party and its alliance partners won 41% of votes and captured the government. The BNP's alliance partners in the 2001 election included the Jamaat-e-Islami (JI), the Islamiya Okiya Jote (IOJ), and the Jatiya Party (JP)—Manzur Faction. They were opposed by the Hasina-led Awami League, which won 40% of the vote at that time. This is the same percentage that the opposition to the present AL government currently has.[14] Elections in Bangladesh are to be held every five years. Bangladesh has instituted a provision for the president to appoint an interim government in the immediate lead-up to polls in order to prevent the incumbent government from using the powers of office to its unfair political advantage.

Bangladesh Politics

Although the December 2008 elections were "well administered and conducted in an orderly fashion" and returned Bangladesh to democratic government, there is some concern that street protests may return to once again become a regular part of the political landscape.[15] A key challenge is to ensure the proper functioning of parliament with an opposition that works within the political framework rather than resorting to street protests. Maintaining an accommodation with the army, which reportedly wants to limit civilian oversight, will remain another challenge for the government. The Brussels-based International Crisis Group has identified a number of challenges facing Bangladesh, including "weak judicial and law enforcement agencies, ethnic conflict, poor relations with regional neighbors, poverty, illiteracy and low development indicators," as well as "militant Islamist groups" and a continuing "culture of impunity" for crimes perpetrated by security forces and senior politicians.[16]

Observers have noted efforts by the AL to press their advantage since their landslide electoral victory in the 2008 election to further weaken the BNP and marginalize Islamist parties, particularly the Jamaat-e-Islami. The Economist Intelligence Unit has identified several key objectives of the current AL government. These include its decision to pursue closer relations with India, plans to prosecute war crimes associated with the 1971 war of independence from West Pakistan, a return to "core values" in the 1972 constitution (which includes the prohibition of religious-based political parties), and an investigation into an attack against AL political leaders at a rally in 2004. Some believe that AL moves against Jamaat-e-Islami and other religious based parties, both through the ban and the war crimes trials, could provoke a backlash and undermine political stability.[17] It has been reported that Bangladesh will ban religious organizations including Hizbut Tawhid, Ad-Din Bangladesh, Liberate Youth, and Allah'r Dal. Islami Okiya Jote, Jamiatul Ulama Bangladesh, and Markajul Islam have also been placed on a list of suspicious organizations.[18]

War Crimes Trials

The AL government passed a resolution to initiate prosecutions of war crimes dating back to the 1971 Bangladesh war of secession and independence. This is viewed as a move that can help the AL further consolidate its political advantage, as it was largely members of the Islamist parties, who have previously been in coalition with the BNP, that were involved in the atrocities. An estimated 3 million people were killed during the 1971 war that was fought between independence forces in then East Pakistan, with assistance from India, and the Pakistani army that was largely composed of troops from then West Pakistan. The trials are aimed at those in Bangladesh who committed war crimes, many of whom are thought to have supported West Pakistan against the Bengali nationalists. Suspects include leading members of the Jamaat-eIslami Party, which is the largest Islamist political party in Bangladesh. Jamaat had a paramilitary wing, Al-Badr, that collaborated with the West Pakistani military during the war for independence and is thought to have assassinated journalists and academics sympathetic to Bengali independence. [19]

THE MILITARY

It appears at present that the government does have the support of the military despite concerns raised by the mutiny by the Bangladesh Rifles (BDR) border security force in February 2009. Corruption, poor pay, and poor benefits apparently led members of the BDR to mutiny on February 25, 2009, and kill 57 BDR officers and 15 of their family members. The two-day mutiny was quickly suppressed by the army, from whose ranks many of the leading officers of the BDR are drawn. Trials of an estimated 3,500 BDR mutineers from this incident are ongoing. [20]

In February 2010, 300 opposition student activist supporters of Islami Chhatra Shibir were rounded up in Dhaka and elsewhere in the country by the military. Islami Chhatra Shibir is the student wing of the opposition Jamaat-e-Islami political party. The arrests followed violence between Islami Chhatra Shibir and the student wing of the AL, who were fighting for control of student residence halls.[21] This apparent use of the military for what could be viewed as a political objective would seem to indicate continuing political control of the military.

The government recently initiated the withdrawal of military forces from the Chittagong Hill Tracts region. This is a key step to implementing a 1997 peace agreement that includes greater autonomy for local tribal peoples. A 20-year insurgency by the Shanti Bahini, which is the military arm of the Parbatya Chattagram Jana Sanghati Samiti (PCJSS), led to the death of 8,500 troops and rebels.[22]

The power behind the former caretaker government is thought by some to have resided with the Directorate General of Forces Intelligence (DGFI). Observers believe the military sought to exert its influence from behind the scenes through the interim caretaker government. Former Army Chief General Moeen Ahmed often reiterated under the caretaker government his pledge that the military had no political ambition and that it was committed to the political roadmap to hold elections by the end of 2008. He also added at that time that the army wished to see honest and competent leadership come to power.[23] Many observers believe that the military wanted to rid Bangladesh of past corrupt leaders and to then withdraw from politics in a way that would preserve the military's position in society and avoid retaliation by disaffected politicians. The extent to which there was uniform support for this objective within the armed forces is unclear.[24]

The difficulty that the military had in dealing with economic difficulties, natural disasters, and the "minus two" strategy of removing Hasina and Zia reportedly undermined the morale of some in the armed forces and led to internal tensions within the military. There reportedly was a split within the officer corps between senior and junior officers with the latter group believing that senior officers have been corrupted through their involvement in the political process.[25]

It has been argued that the military is restrained by a desire not to jeopardize its lucrative involvement in international peacekeeping. Bangladesh first became involved in United Nations peacekeeping in 1988 and has since contributed some 60,000 soldiers to such efforts. Bangladesh had some 9,600 soldiers serving abroad in U.N. peace operations in 11 different countries in March 2008, making Bangladesh one of the largest sources of U.N. troops.[26] It has been reported that the U.N. resident representative in Bangladesh has in the past pointed out that the military's actions in Bangladesh have implications for its involvement in U.N. peacekeeping contracts.[27] Bangladeshi troops have a reputation for being disciplined and have fewer complaints lodged against them than U.N. troops from many other countries.[28]

ISLAMIST EXTREMISM

Bangladesh was originally founded on secular-socialist principles and firmly grounded in an ethnic Bengali nationalism as opposed to a Muslim religious identity. Some have attributed the rise of Islamist influence in Bangladesh to the failure of Bangladeshi political elites to effectively govern. This has been described as a crisis of hegemony of the rulers who have failed to provide moral leadership or effectively represent the interests of the masses.[29] Many believe this has created political space for the Islamists to gain influence.

The political context for the potential influence of Islamist extremism is demonstrated by the role that Islamist parties played as coalition partners in the previous BNP government. The BNP government of Khaleda Zia ruled with coalition support from the Jamaat Islami (JI) and Islami Okiya Jote (IOJ) political parties. These two political parties have an Islamist political agenda and are thought to have ties to radical extremists.[30]

Because of the near-even electoral balance between the BNP and the AL in the pre-2007 political environment, the Islamist political parties, JI and IOJ in particular, enjoyed political influence disproportionate to their support among the Bangladeshi electorate. The current split within the BNP appears to be creating a more multi-party system in which Islamist political parties may not enjoy the same degree of influence. Some analysts believe the parties' abilities to be political queen-makers may be less obvious with more potential political factions and parties. Islamists rioted in Dhaka in April 2008 to protest a draft law that would give equal inheritance rights to women. This triggered further protests in Chittagong on April 11 in which Islamist activists, many of them reportedly madrasa students, attacked a police station.[31]

The previous caretaker government indicated its resolve to fight Islamist extremism by executing six leaders of the Islamist extremist group Jamaatul Mujahideen Bangladesh (JMB) in March 2007. The previous BNP government also demonstrated newfound resolve to fight terrorism despite having Islamist political parties in its coalition.

Extremist Groups

Several militant extremist groups operate in Bangladesh, including Harkat ul Jihad al Islami (HuJi), Jagrata Muslim Janata Bangladesh (JMJB), and

Jama'atul Mujahideen Bangladesh (JMB). Some Bangladeshi observers have alleged that the presence in the former ruling Bangladesh National Party (BNP) Coalition government of two Islamist parties, the Islamiya Okiyya Jote (IOJ) and the Jamaat-e-Islami, expanded Islamist influence in Bangladesh and created space within which terrorist and extremist groups could operate. Islami Okiyya Jote is reported to have ties to the radical Harkat-ul-Jihad-al-Islami (HuJI).[32] Jamaat may also have had ties to Harkat ul-Jihad-i-Islami, which itself has ties to Al Qaeda. Harkat leader Fazlul Rahman signed an Osama bin Laden holy war declaration in 1998.[33] JMB seeks the imposition of Sharia law for Bangladesh and is thought responsible for the widespread and coordinated August 2005 bombings. HuJI has been implicated in the January 2002 attack on the American Center in Calcutta, India.[34] HuJI, or the Movement of Islamic Holy War, is on the U.S. State Department's list of "other terrorist organizations" and is thought to have links to Pakistani militant groups. It is also thought to have a cadre strength of several thousand.[35] Awami League sources claimed that former fundamentalist leader Bangla Bhai had ties to Jamaat-e-Islami.[36] AL leader Sheikh Hasina has accused the previous government of "letting loose communal extremist forces."[37] Some news sources have reported that international extremists have used Bangladeshi passports and that some have obtained them with the assistance of sympathetic officials at various Bangladesh embassies under the previous government.[38]

Two senior members of IOJ have reportedly been connected with the reemergence of Harkat ul Jihad (HuJi) under the name "Conscious Islamic People."[39] It has also been reported that the political wing of HuJi may seek to enter politics under the name Islami Gono Andolon.[40] The former BNP government had denied the presence of significant terrorist elements in the country and reportedly had even expelled BNP lawmaker Abu Hena from the BNP for speaking out against extremist activities at a time when the official view was that such extremists did not exist.[41]

The former BNP government eventually moved to suppress the Jamaat-ul-Mujahideen (JMB) and the Jagrata Muslim Janata Bangladesh (JMJB) terrorist groups operating in Bangladesh. The government sentenced to death JMB leaders Shaikh Abdur Rahman and Siddiq ul Islam, also known as "Bangla Bhai," as well as five other JMB members, in May 2006. They were subsequently executed for their role in the bombings.[42] The two Islamist militant leaders received their sentences for the murder of two judges in November of 2005. They are also believed to have been behind widespread bombings in Bangladesh and to have sought to replace the secular legal system with Sharia law through such attacks. The government also reportedly has arrested some 900 lower-level militants, 7 known senior leaders, 4 out of 11 commanders, and some 20 district leaders on terrorism charges.[43] Despite this, the then-leader of the opposition, Sheikh Hassina, stated "militants are partners of the government ... the government catches a few militants whenever foreign guests visit Bangladesh." She has also alleged that Jamaat has 15,000 guerillas and its own training camps. Hassina has also stated that the arrest of JMB operatives is "only the tip of the iceberg."[44]

It appears that the former BNP government shifted its position on the necessity of acknowledging and addressing Islamist militants in August of 2005. In response, JMB leader Rahman reportedly stated, "masks will fall and you [the authorities] will be exposed." Such an allegation is consistent with allegations by the AL, which accused the former BNP government, or more likely elements within the government, of allowing Islamist militancy to rise in Bangladesh.[45]

Selig Harrison, a prominent South Asia analyst, noted in early August 2006 that "a growing Islamic fundamentalist movement linked to al-Qaeda and Pakistani intelligence agencies is steadily converting the strategically located nation of Bangladesh into a new regional hub for terrorist operations that reach into India and Southeast Asia." Harrison pointed out that former Prime Minister Khaleda Zia's Bangladesh National Party's coalition alliance with the Jamaat-eIslami Party of Bangladesh led to a "Faustian bargain" that brought Jamaat officials into the government. These officials, he argued, in turn allowed Taliban-styled squads to operate with impunity. Jamaat's entry into the former BNP government also reportedly led to fundamentalist control over large parts of the Bangladesh economy, Islamist madrassa schools acting as fronts for terrorist activity, fundamentalist inroads being made in the armed forces, and rigging (by manipulating voter lists) of the elections that were originally scheduled for January 2007.[46]

On July 11, 2006, a series of coordinated bomb blasts killed approximately 200 persons while wounding some 500 others on commuter trains in Bombay (Mumbai), India. Indian authorities subsequently arrested several individuals reportedly with ties to terrorist groups in Bangladesh and Nepal who were "directly or indirectly" linked to Pakistan. Indian intelligence officials have portrayed the bombers as being backed by Pakistan-supported terrorist groups. Pakistan has denied these allegations.[47] Allegations had been made that the explosives had come from Bangladesh. In response, Bangladesh authorities stated that the Jamaat ul-Mujahideen (JMB) attacks in Bangladesh on August 17, 2005, which killed 30 in a series of nationwide blasts, were of Indian origin.[48] Six of the eight arrested in India in connection with the bombings are thought to have received training from Lashkar-e-Toiba at terrorist camps in Pakistan. Lashkar is a Pakistan-based, Al Queda-allied terrorist group.

Although most of the terrorism focus in India has been on Pakistan, Bharatiya Janata Party (BJP) President Rajnath Singh has called on the Indian government to pressure Bangladesh to dismantle terrorist training centers in Bangladesh. The Hindu nationalist BJP is the leading opposition party in India. Singh also stated that Bangladesh had become "a centre of Islamic fundamentalist forces."[49] The anti-terrorism squad investigating the Bombay blasts also interrogated a number of individuals in a village in Tripura, India, that borders Bangladesh.[50] A bombing in Varanasi, India, in March 2006 also reportedly had links to HuJi in Bangladesh.[51]

Army forces captured Habibur Rahman Bulbuli in June 2007. Bulbuli was leader of the Khelafat Majlish that is a component of the Islamiya Okiya Jote, which was a junior partner in the former BNP government of Khaleda Zia. Bulbuli has claimed to be a veteran of fighting in Afghanistan and a follower of Osama bin Laden.[52] In June 2007, Bangladesh police charged Mufti Hannan and three accomplices, who are all now in prison, with trying to assassinate the British High Commissioner Anwar Choudhury in 2004. Choudhury, who is of Bangladeshi origin, was wounded in a grenade attack as were some 50 others. Three were also killed in the attack, which occurred at a shrine near Choudhury's ancestral home.[53] The Rapid Action Battalion (RAB) reportedly captured four suspected members of Jamaat-ul-Mujahideen, as well as grenades and explosives, near Kishoregani northwest of Dhaka on July 18, 2007.[54]

Recent Action against Militants

Bangladesh has been largely successful in destabilizing Islamist militants since the widespread bombings of 2005 that were carried out by the militant group Jamaat-ul-Mujahideen Bangladesh (JMB). Hundreds of JMB members, including key leaders, were arrested, and the leadership, including JMB founder Shaikh Abdur Rahman, were executed in the aftermath of the 2005 bombings. Rahman sought to establish Islamist rule in Bangladesh. Continuing arrests and seizures of bomb-making materials in recent years suggest that despite the crackdown on militants since 2005 JMB had been able to regroup, at least to a limited extent. Recent reports of ongoing JMB linkages to the Pakistani based Lashkar-e-Taiba (LeT) and British based al Muhajiroun, as well as financial sympathizers in Saudi Arabia and Kuwait, are a cause of concern that JMB may have the resources to further regroup.[55] The United States is supportive of Bangladesh efforts against Islamist militants.[56] There are reports that Harkatul Jihad (HuJi) and the Rohingya Solidarity Organization (RSO) of Burma have the objective of creating an Islamic state in the area of Burma's Arakan state and Bangladesh areas around Cox's Bazaar, Bandarban and South Chittagong. It has also been reported that HuJi and RSO may have ties to Pakistan intelligence.[57] It was reported that five operatives of Jaish-e-Muhammad, including a Pakistani national, were arrested by the Rapid Action Battalion (RAB) in Dhaka in March 2010.[58]

BANGLADESH-U. S. RELATIONS

U.S. policy toward Bangladesh emphasizes support for political stability and democracy, development, and human rights with some military-to-military exchanges as well. The United States has long-standing supportive relations with Bangladesh and views Bangladesh as a moderate voice in the Islamic world. U.S. Pacific Command works closely with Bangladesh to help expand and improve Bangladesh's peacekeeping, humanitarian assistance, disaster relief, and maritime security capabilities. Pacific Command views Bangladesh as a "strong partner who works closely with the U.S. to enhance regional security," which is also committed to improving their counterterrorism capability.[59]

Bangladesh is a very poor country where an estimated 80% of the population live on less than $2 per day. The U.S. State Department views U.S. assistance as vital to strengthening the country after its return to a democratically elected government. The Foreign Operations budget request for Bangladesh typically seeks to support long-term development in Bangladesh by "addressing the underlying social, demographic, and economic factors that inhibit economic growth and increase vulnerability to extremism." U.S. assistance can be broken down into the categories of peace and security, governing justly and democratically, investing in people, supporting economic growth, humanitarian assistance, and program support.[60]

U.S. Democratic Strengthening Programs

The State Department 2011 Budget Justification Document discusses U.S. assistance to Bangladesh by both account and objective. The accounts are specified in Table 1 below. Drawing from different accounts, a total of $24,602,000 was requested for the objective of Governing Justly and Democratically in 2011. This would represent an increase of $1,340,000 over the estimated 2010 budget. Such assistance would go to Rule of Law and Human Rights, Good Governance, Political Competition and Consensus Building, and Civil Society programs. Funds for Governing Justly and Democratically would largely be drawn from International Narcotics Control and Law Enforcement and Development Assistance accounts and would address issues such as "legislative and technical support to improve prosecutorial and judicial reform ... supporting Bangladesh's ongoing transition to a fully functional democracy by strengthening key democratic practices and institutions ... transparency and accountability in Government ... focus on civil society development ... reinforcing the media's watchdog function [and through] ... the promotion of basic human rights." [61]

**Table 1. U.S. Foreign Assistance to Bangladesh
By Account and Fiscal Year ($s in thousands)**

	FY2009 actual	FY2010 estimate	FY2011 request
Development Assistance	40,000	66,271	81,902
Economic Support Fund	50,000	0	0
Food for Peace	30,029	42,000	42,000
Foreign Military Financing	590	1,500	1,500
Global Health and Child Survival	41,550	53,200	77,300
International Military Education & Training	787	1,000	1,000
International Narcotics Control & Law Enforcement	200	350	850
Nonproliferation, Antiterrorism, Demining and related Programs	3,600	4,200	2,575
Total	166,756	168,521	207,127

Source: U.S. State Department, "Bangladesh," Budget Justification Document, 2011.

One area for possible additional U.S. assistance for Bangladesh would be in the area of the environment and climate change adaptation and mitigation assistance, as the consequences of climate change for this low-lying nation may increase dramatically in the years ahead. (See "Environmental Concerns, Climate Change, and Food Security" section below.) U.S. Agency for International Development (USAID) is working with Bangladesh on a multi-stakeholder approach that uses a co-management model to link management authorities and local communities to achieve sustainable natural resource management and biodiversity conservation. Two USAID pilot projects have been carried out. These pilot projects focused on the Management of Aquatic Ecosystems Through Community Husbandry and the Co-Management of Tropical Forest Resources. Under provisions in the U.S. Tropical Forest Conservation Act the government of Bangladesh and the U.S. government have agreed to pursue a debt-for-nature swap to promote tropical forest conservation in Bangladesh. [62]

BANGLADESH IN A REGIONAL CONTEXT

Bangladesh is a nation of strategic importance not only to the South Asian sub-region but to the larger geopolitical dynamics of Asia as a whole. The Bengalis' struggle with West Pakistan was at the center of the 1971 Indo-Pakistan war. The creation of the independent state of Bangladesh at that time forever weakened Pakistan's position relative to India. This has enabled India to operate as a key actor not only in South Asia, but in Asia as a whole. As a result, India could potentially challenge and/or balance China's emerging strategic posture in Asia. In this way, Bangladesh has played, and will likely continue to play, a role in the shifting regional balance of power between India and China. Some Bangladeshi strategic thinkers believe that China should now be pursued as a strategic counterweight to Bangladesh's relationship with India. The recent opening of road and rail routes through Chittagong and Mangla ports in Bangladesh to India's northeast has led others in Bangladesh to talk of developing trade linkages to China.[63]

Bangladesh-China Relations

Prime Minister Hasina traveled to China in March 2010 to seek closer cooperation with China in a number of areas. These include Chinese cooperation to construct a deep sea port at Chittagong and to establish a road link from Chittagong to Kunming, China. Bilateral trade between Bangladesh and China is expected to increase to $5 billion in 2010 from $4.58 billion in 2009.[64] Some have also called for Chinese investment in developing a deep seaport at Sonadia near Cox's Bazaar, which is relatively close to Bangladesh's border with Burma, and using Kunming-Burma road linkages.[65]

A "Closer Comprehensive Partnership of Cooperation" joint statement was issued on March 19, 2010, to take bilateral relations between China and Bangladesh forward. The statement called for intensifying cooperation in a number of areas that include sharing hydrological information on the Brahmaputra, intensifying exchanges, Chinese dredging of river beds, enhancing transportation links, increasing bilateral trade, and strengthening exchange and cooperation between the two states' militaries "to safeguard respective national security and stability and promote peace and stability in the region." Bangladesh reaffirmed its One China policy and expressed support for China's efforts to enhance its cooperation with South Asian Association of Regional Cooperation (SARC) countries.[66]

Ongoing engagement by China with South Asian states, particularly in the area of developing port access, has led to suspicion of China's motives among some in strategic circles in India and the United States. From this perspective, port development in Bangladesh could be seen as part of a "String of Pearls" strategy that could be used by China to secure sea lanes that cross the Indian Ocean and link its industrialized eastern seaboard with the energy resources of the Middle East. China has been developing ports in Gwadar, Pakistan, and at Hambantota, Sri Lanka, and has expanded its influence in Burma in recent years.

Bangladesh-India Relations

Prime Minister Hasina appears to be pursuing improved relations with India as well as with China. India supported Bangladesh's struggle for independence from West Pakistan, of which Bangladesh was a part from 1947 to 1971. Despite this, relations between India and Bangladesh have been strained at times due to border disputes, the presence of Islamist militants in

Bangladesh, and Indian concern that insurgents from India's northeast have sought refuge inside Bangladesh.

Bangladesh's land borders are almost entirely with India with the exception of a short border with Burma. It is reported that 68 Bangladeshis were killed in the first three months of 2010 by Indian Border Security Forces (BSF). There was also a clash between India's BSF and the Bangladesh Rifles (BDR) along the border in March 2010 that injured 18.[67] There are also areas of improvement in border relations between the two states. Bangladesh recently opened Chittagong port to Indian exports.

Relations have improved in recent years as Bangladesh suppressed Islamist militants and returned Hasina's Awami League to office. The AL is perceived in India as relatively better disposed to India than the BNP. Relations improved further after Prime Minister Hasina's visit to India in January 2010. During that visit several agreements were signed including one on combating international terrorism. The Annual Report of the Indian Ministry of Defence (MOD) released in March 2010 reportedly states that "relations with Bangladesh have been strengthened since the restoration of multiparty democracy ... India is appreciative of the increasing cooperation with Bangladesh in security matters, especially vis-à-vis Indian insurgent groups operating from its territory."[68] India also announced a $1 billion line of credit for a range of projects for Bangladesh at that time. [69]

There are reports of increasing tensions between India and China over border disputes including India's border with China in Arunchal Pradesh to the north of Bangladesh. The MOD report stated "necessary steps have been initiated for the upgrading of our infrastructure and force structuring along the northern borders."[70] Bangladesh's apparent policy to develop closer ties with both India and China may have difficulty should tensions mount between India and China.

HUMAN RIGHTS

The human rights situation in Bangladesh "improved somewhat" with the return of elected government in 2009 but also led to a slight increase in extra-judicial killing and a 3.3% increase in politically motivated violence. Areas of concern in 2009 included "extrajudicial killings, custodial deaths, arbitrary arrest and detention, and harassment of journalists." The February 2009 mutiny by members of the Bangladesh Rifles (BDR) border force led to the death in custody of 59 BDR soldiers out of some 2,000 that were arrested for their role in the mutiny. There were reports that many of the dead were tortured.[71] While Islam is the state religion by constitution in Bangladesh, religious freedom is also guaranteed by the constitution, but attacks against religious minority groups continue. The secular approach of the AL has gained it the support of religious minority groups in Bangladesh.[72]

In 2008 the state of human rights in Bangladesh remained of concern because of the continued suspension of democratic government. According to the State Department, "although levels of violence declined significantly and the caretaker government oversaw successful elections, the government's human rights record remained a matter of serious concern, in part due to the state of emergency that remained in place for much of the year" of 2008.[73]

The Rohingya

The Rohingya, a Mulsim ethnic group from Burma's western Arakan state, have sought refuge in Bangladesh for decades. The most recent Rohingya refugees include an estimated 250,000 to 260,000 who fled Burma in 1991-1992. In 2010, it was estimated by one source that 400,000 Burmese nationals, most of whom belong to the Rohingya group, were in Bangladesh, predominantly in the Cox's Bazaar district, along with approximately 28,000 Rohingya who are registered as refugees and are living in a United Nations camp. Another source estimated the number of Rohingya in Bangladesh in 2010 to be 220,000 with an additional 700,000 Rohingya still in Burma. The United Nations High Commissioner for Refugees (UNHCR) has sought to assist the repatriation of the Rohingya. Since 2006 it has resettled 749 Rohingya from those in the registered camp in Bangladesh to third countries.[74]

It has been reported that Bangladesh initiated a crackdown in 2009-2010 that led to the arrest of over 500 Rohingya, pushed an estimated 6,000 Rohingyas into the Kutu-Palong camp near the border with Burma, and pushed an additional 2,000 back over the border into Burma.[75] Bangladesh has also reportedly sought the assistance of China to influence Burma to take back the Rohingya refugees. Burma reportedly agreed to take back 9,000 of the 28,000 refugees in December 2009.[76]

ECONOMIC DEVELOPMENT AND TRADE

Bangladesh's GDP is expected to grow by 5.7% in 2010 following 5.9% growth in 2009.[77] The global economic downturn has reduced demand for Bangladesh exports. Merchandise exports decreased 7.7% year on year as of November 2009.[78] In April 2009, the government announced a $500 million stimulus package to spur economic growth and placed emphasis on public-private partnerships.[79] The United States and Bangladesh have had discussions over the possibility of a Trade and Investment Framework Agreement (TIFA) or a U.S.-Bangladesh Economic and Trade Cooperation Forum (UBETCF). Bangladesh would like to increase market access for its products in the United States.[80]

There are an estimated 6 million Bangladeshis working abroad. They are estimated to have sent $9.7 billion to Bangladesh in 2008-2009, making Bangladesh one of the world's largest sources of overseas workers. This represents an increase of 22.4% year on year. Remittances are a significant source of revenue and are expected to decline in 2009-2010 due to the global economic downturn.[81]

Energy

Bangladesh is currently experiencing a shortfall in energy as demand exceeds supply. Despite energy reserves, Bangladesh is experiencing an estimated daily shortfall of 300 million cubic feet of gas and 2,000 megawatts of electricity.[82] Bangladesh has a world rank of 32nd in natural gas production, with an annual output of 17.9 billion cubic meters, and ranks 48th in proven reserves with 141.6 billion cubic meters.[83] Bangladesh is also thought to have 3.3 billion tons of estimated coal reserves. It has been estimated that Bangladesh needs $12 billion in investment over the next five years to meet demand for energy that is growing at an annual rate of 8% to 10%.

Chevron Corporation is reported to be conducting seismic surveys near its operations in the Jalalabad gas fields following reports that indicate larger reserves than had previously been thought to exist in the area. Chevron has been extracting hydrocarbon from the field since 1999 reportedly without loss in pressure.[84] Chevron produces approximately 45% of Bangladesh's gas output and is reportedly optimistic that additional reserves will be found since Bangladesh's energy potential is relatively unexplored.[85]

There appear to be problems with the government's recent efforts to fast track gas exploration in state-owned offshore gas fields that may contain substantial reserves. The government's hydrocarbon unit is expected to increase estimates of Bangladesh's gas reserves.[86]

ENVIRONMENTAL CONCERNS, CLIMATE CHANGE, AND FOOD SECURITY

Bangladesh is one of the countries of the world thought most likely to suffer the adverse effects of climate change. Some view it as the most vulnerable country to the negative impact of climate change, due to its low-lying geography.[87] Adverse impacts of climate change already observed in Bangladesh include damage to infrastructure due to natural disasters that may be caused by climate change, saltwater intrusion leading to the damage of 830,000 hectares of cultivatable land, river bank erosion leading to more damaging floods, too little water during the dry season, and too much water during the monsoon leading to declining agricultural output.[88]

Rising sea levels and increased salinity in low-lying areas are thought to be responsible for undermining forest health and leading to lower crop yields. The Intergovernmental Panel on Climate Change (IPCC) has projected that rice and wheat production in Bangladesh could decrease by 8% and 32% respectively by the year 2050 and that rice yields will likely decrease by 10% for every one degree Celsius rise in growing-season minimum temperature.[89] Farmers in coastal areas have either had to move to cities or adapt through such measures as switching from growing rice to farming prawns due to increased salinity of water. Bangladesh has reportedly developed a new strain of rice that will grow in salty water. Bangladesh government perspectives on climate change are detailed in the 2008 *Bangladesh Climate Change Strategy and Action Plan* document.[90] Bangladesh plans to hold a regional climate change conference in May or June 2010.[91]

Projected decreases in crop yields due to climate change and an increasing population when combined with Bangladesh's limited economic resources mean that the nation has only limited resilience to deal with further stresses on its environment. This was made evident in the aftermath of the Cyclone *Sidr* which killed 3,000 to 6,000 in Bangladesh in November 2007 while destroying nearly 2 to 3 million tons of rice in the fields in Bangladesh.[92] Bangladesh's total rice harvest equaled 27 million tons in 2007.[93]

Population growth leads to increased demand for rice. Although Bangladesh's rate of growth is declining, its overall population is still increasing. Bangladesh's population growth rate declined from 3.4% in 1975 to 2.2% in 1991 and was 1.9% in 1996.[94] It is currently 1.29%.[95] Bangladesh does not appear to have the capacity to significantly increase its agricultural output, as higher- yielding varieties of rice have already been introduced and it appears that most all land suitable for rice production is already being used. One estimate has projected that Bangladesh's population could nearly double to 300 million, or about the total current U.S. population, by 2050.[96] Other projections are less dire and estimate Bangladesh's population growth reaching a total population of 231 million by 2050.[97]

Rice is critical for food security in Bangladesh as it accounts for 75% of the calories in Bangladeshis' diet. Rice also accounts for 75% of cropped land and contributes 92% of total foodgrains produced in Bangladesh. Almost all cultivatable land is already in use in Bangladesh. Soil degradation may require high expenditures on agricultural inputs to make up for decreasing fertility of soils. As a result, it has been projected that "Bangladesh will face an enormous challenge by 2020 in trying to achieve food self reliance and to ensure food security for all."[98] Increasing urbanization also means that a higher percentage of the population is affected by price increases as they no longer produce their own rice. The urban population is also located closer to the centres of power in Dhaka.

Such a large dependence on rice means that it is critical to political stability as well. An estimated 20,000 workers rioted near Dhaka in 2008 over food prices, particularly the cost of rice, which soared in the aftermath of two floods and Cyclone *Sidr* in Bangladesh in 2007. These weather events led to a doubling of the price of rice in Bangladesh in 2008 and meant that food costs accounted for 70% of the average Bangladeshi household's income.[99] A food security/political security paradigm adds the additional requirement that rice not only be available but that it be available at an affordable price for Bangladeshis in order that it not become a politically destabilizing issue.

Bangladesh reached food self sufficiency in the 1 990s due largely to the introduction of "green revolution" technologies and higher-yielding varieties of rice. [100] Despite this, Bangladesh is once again importing rice. The government reportedly imported 4 million tons of rice from India in the six months preceding April 2008, twice the level of the year before. [101] Such imports become a significant drain on Bangladesh's economy.

Climate change appears to have resolved a maritime dispute between India and Bangladesh as one of the islands disputed by the two states has disappeared beneath the sea. New Moore Island in the Sundarbans has now submerged and 10 other islands in the area are thought to be at risk.

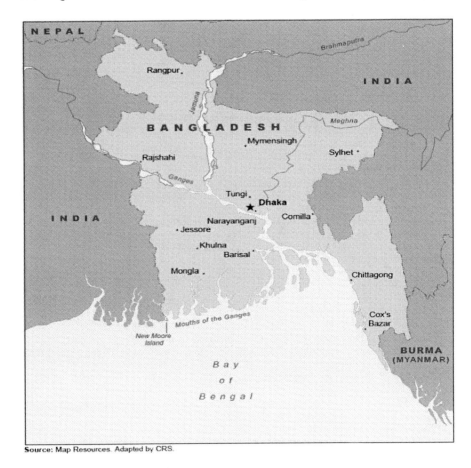

Figure 1. Map of Bangladesh

One estimate projects that 18% of Bangladesh's coastal area will be underwater by 2050, displacing 20 million people, if sea levels rise by 1 meter as projected by some climate models.[102] Bangladesh's Foreign Minister Dipu Moni has stated that up to one-third of Bangladesh could be lost to sea level rise induced by climate change.[103] Bangladesh's lack of resources to accommodate such climate refugees, and already stressed conditions due to extreme population density, could lead to cross-border migrations into bordering India, which could exacerbate existing border tensions. Bangladesh has a population density of about 949 people per square kilometer as compared with the United States with 30, and Australia with 2.5 people per square kilometer. There are approximately 2.6 square kilometers and 640 acres in a square mile. [104] As a result, it is already pushing the outer limits of what the land and the natural resources of the nation can sustain.

End Notes

[1] "Background Note: Bangladesh," Department of State, May 2009.
[2] Zahurul Alam, "US Congress Delegation in Bangladesh Pushes for a Strong Democracy," *Voice of America*, March 29, 2010.
[3] "Dhaka Open to Any Move 'Alternative to TIFA," *The Financial Express*, March 13, 2010.
[4] Secretary of State Hillary Clinton, "Remarks with Bangladesh Foreign Minister Dipu Moni After Their Meeting," September 16, 2009.
[5] "Monthly Report: Ranking of Military and Police Contributions to UN Operations," United Nations, December 31, 2009.
[6] Bureau of Democracy, Human Rights, and Labor, 2008 Country Reports on Human Rights Practices, "Bangladesh," February 25, 2009.
[7] "Bangladesh Today," *International Crisis Group*, October 23, 2006.
[8] The Department of State, Congressional Budget Justification Document, 2011.
[9] "MiG-29 Purchase Case: Hasina Graft Charges Quashed," Notes From Bangla Paper, March 10, 2010.
[10] Maneeza Hossain, "Broken Pendulum: Bangladesh's Swing to Radicalism," *The Hudson Institute*, 2007.
[11] Roland Buerk, "Bangladesh and Islamic Militants," *BBC News*, February 25, 2005.
[12] Devin Hagerty, "Bangladesh in 2007," *Asian Survey*, February 2008.
[13] "Background Notes: Bangladesh," Department of State, Bureau of South and Central Asian Affairs, May 2007.
[14] Bangladesh elects its representatives by district. CIA, *The World Factbook*, http://www.cis.gov/cia/publications/ factbook/geos/bg.
[15] "NDI Delegation Finds Bangladesh Parliamentary Elections Well Administered and Peaceful," *National Democratic Institute*, http://www.ndi.org.
[16] "Bangladesh," International Crisis Group, http://www.crisisgroup.org.
[17] "Bangladesh Politics: Power Shift," *The Economist Intelligence Unit*, January 22, 2010.
[18] "Four Religious Organizations to be Banned," *Samakal*, March 3, 2010, from Notes from Bangla Newspapers.
[19] "Bangladesh Politics: Do Mention the War," *The Economist*, July 23, 2009.
[20] "BDR Peelkhana Mutiny Trial Begins Today," *The Daily Star*, February 23, 2010.
[21] "Politically Motivated Arbitrary Arrests Hamper Impartial Investigation of Campus Violence," *Amnesty International*, February 23, 2010.
[22] "Country Report Bangladesh," *The Economist Intelligence Unit*, August 2009.
[23] "No Deviation From Electoral Roadmap, Says Gen. Moeen," *United News of Bangladesh*, April 11, 2008.
[24] *Country Report: Bangladesh*, The Economist Intelligence Unit, May 2008.
[25] "Restoring Democracy in Bangladesh," *International Crisis Group*, April 28, 2008.
[26] "2,728 Bangladeshi Peacekeepers Decorated with UN Medal," *Independent Bangladesh*, March 31, 2008.
[27] "The UN in Bangladesh," *The Economist*, February 21, 2007.
[28] Roland Buerk, "The Cream of UN Peacekeepers," *BBC News*, January 18, 2006.

[29] Ali Riaz, *God Willing: The Politics of Islamism in Bangladesh* (New York: Rowman and Littlefield Publishers, 2004).
[30] See CRS Report RL33646, *Bangladesh: Background and U.S. Relations*, by Bruce Vaughn, for additional background information.
[31] "Authorities Order Intensified Security Vigil in Dhaka," *Press Trust of India*, April 12, 2008. See CRS Report RS22591, *Islamist Extremism in Bangladesh*, by Bruce Vaughn, for additional background information.
[32] Roland Buerk, "Bangladesh and Islamic Militants," *BBC News*, February 25, 2005.
[33] "Bangladesh Becoming a Regional Terror Hub," *Hindustan Times*, August 3, 2006.
[34] "Bangladesh's First Suicide Bombers," *Janes Terrorism and Security Monitor*, January 18, 2006.
[35] Office of the Coordinator for Counterterrorism, Department of State, *Patterns of Global Terrorism, 2003*, April 29, 2004.
[36] Roland Buerk, "Bangladesh's Escalating Extremism," *BBC News*, November 29, 2005.
[37] Roland Buerk, "Dhaka Struggles to Respond to Bombs," *BBC News*, August 2005.
[38] "International Terrorists Using Bangladeshi Passports," *Notes From the Bangla Media*, August 30, 2006, The U.S. Embassy, Dhaka, "Bangladesh Press Selection," *BBC News*, August 30, 2006; and "BSF Wants Anup Chetia Deported," *Indian Express*, August 29, 2006.
[39] "IOJ Behind Reemergence of Harkatul Jihad," Notes From the Bangla Media, United States Embassy, Dhaka, August 22, 2006.
[40] "War on Terror Digest 21-22 Aug 06," *BBC Monitoring*, August 22, 2006.
[41] "Summer of Discontent in the BNP," *United News of Bangladesh*, June 9, 2006.
[42] "Bangladesh Arrests Two Senior Leaders of Banned Militant Group," *BBC News*, July 12, 2007.
[43] "Bangladesh Coalition Partners to Face Election Together Amid Terrorism Charges," *Open Source Center*, July 13, 2006.
[44] "Militants Arrest Meant to Impress US: Hassina," *Hindustan Times*, August 4, 2006.
[45] "Bangladesh Blast Masterminds Sentenced to Death," *Agence France-Presse*, May 29, 2006.
[46] Selig Harrison, "A New Hub for Terrorism? In Bangladesh, An Islamic Movement with Al-Qaeda Ties is on the Rise," *Washington Post*, August 2, 2006.
[47] "Three Arrested Over Mumbai Bombs Linked to Pakistan," *Financial Times*, August 6, 2006.
[48] Waliur Rahman, "Dhaka Dismisses Mumbai Bomb Claim," *BBC News*, July 15, 2006.
[49] "Uproot Terror Camps From Bangla: BJP," *Hindustan Times*, July 19, 2006.
[50] "Mumbai Police Interrogates Terror Suspects in Tripura," *Hindustan Times*, July 19, 2006.
[51] "Bangla Immigrants the Threat Within," *Times of India*, July 14, 2006.
[52] "Bangladesh Forces Capture Afghan War Veteran Bulbuli," *Asia News International*, May 16, 2007.
[53] "B'desh Charges Islamists for Attacks on U.K. Envoy," *Reuters*, June 9, 2007.
[54] "Bangladesh Arrests Islamists, Seizes Explosives," *Reuters*, July 18, 2007.
[55] The Threat From Jamaat-Ul-Mujahideen Bangladesh," *International Crisis Group*, March 1, 2010.
[56] "US Supports Bangladesh's Counterterrorism Approach," *The Daily Star*, March 14, 2010.
[57] "Religious Organizations to be Banned," *Jugantor*, March 3, 2010. From Notes from Bangla Newspapers.
[58] "Five of a Pak-based Militant Outfit Held," *The Independent*, March 3, 2010.
[59] Senate Armed Services Committee Testimony of Robert Willard, Commander, U.S. Pacific Command, March 26, 2010.
[60] United States Department of State, Foreign Operations Congressional Budget Justification Document, "Bangladesh," 2010.
[61] The Department of State, Congressional Budget Justification Document, 2011.
[62] "U.S. AID's Response: Environment," USAID Bangladesh, http://www.usaid.gov.
[63] "Dhaka Should Balance Ties with Delhi, Beijing," *Plus News Pakistan*, March 15, 2010.
[64] "PM Seeks Chinese Assistance to Set Up Deep-Sea Port," *Financial Express*, March 19, 2010.

[65] "Bangladesh: Balacing Ties with Delhi and Beijing," *China Forum*, April 13, 2010, http://bbs.chinadaily.com.
[66] "Dhaka-Beijing Jt Statement Outlines Closer Cooperation," *The Daily Star*, March 20, 2010.
[67] "Shootout at India-Bangladesh Border Injures 18," *Global Insight*, March 15, 2010.
[68] "Fighting Maoists Focus of India's Internal Security," *BBC News*, March 31, 2010.
[69] D. Roy, "Hasina's Visit to India a Landmark Moment," *Mail Today*, March 26, 2010.
[70] "India to 'Restructure' Force Levels Along China Border," *BBC News*, March 30, 2010.
[71] Bureau of Democracy, Human Rights, and Labor, 2008 Country Reports on Human Rights Practices, "Bangladesh," March 11, 2010.
[72] Bureau of Democracy, Human Rights, and Labor, "Bangladesh," International Religious Freedom Report, October 26, 2009.
[73] Bureau of Democracy, Human Rights, and Labor, 2008 Country Reports on Human Rights Practices, "Bangladesh," February 25, 2009.
[74] Misha Hussain, "For Rohingya in Bangladesh, No Place is Home," *Time*, February 19, 2010.
[75] "Rohingya 'Crackdown' in Bangladesh," *Al Jazeera*, February 18, 2010.
[76] "B'desh Rejects UN Plea to Register Myanmarese as Refugees," *ZEE News*, April 10,20 10.
[77] "Bangladesh: Country Report," *The Economist Intelligence Unit*, April, 2010.
[78] "Bangladesh Economy: Growth Challenge," *The Economist Intelligence Unit*, March 2, 2010.
[79] "Bangladesh Announces $500 mn Recession Relief Package," *ThaiIndian News*, April 19, 2009.
[80] "Moriarty Pushes for TIFA," *The Daily Star*, February 19, 2010.
[81] "Country Report Bangladesh," *The Economist Intelligence Unit*, August 2009.
[82] "IMF Urges Bangladesh to Raise Power Production," *Euclid Infotech*, April 13, 2010.
[83] CIA World Factbook, "Country Comparison: Natural Gas," http://www.cia.gov.
[84] "Chevron Expects Jalalabad to Contain Bigger Gas Reserves," *Euclid Infotech*, April 12, 2010.
[85] "Chevron Boss for drilling More Wells in Unexplored Areas," *The Financial Express*, March 25, 2010.
[86] "Gas Reserves Being Reassessed," *Jugantor*, Notes from the Bangla Papers, March 10, 2010.
[87] Devin Hagerty, "Bangladesh in 2007," *Asian Survey*, February 2008.
[88] "Impacts of Climate Change in Bangladesh," August 27, 2009, http://www.climatefrontlines.org.
[89] IPCC, *Climate Change 2007: Working Group II: Impacts, Adaptation and Vulnerability*, 2007.
[90] "Bangladesh: At the Mercy of Climate Change," *The Independent*, February 2007.
[91] "Climate Change Meeting to be Held in Dhaka," Notes from the Bangla Papers, March 10, 2010.
[92] "Cyclone Sidr Response," *Direct Relief International*, February 29, 2008 and "Bangladesh Imports Burma Rice," *The Irrawaddy*, 2008.
[93] Masud Karim, "Bangladesh to Import More Rice," *Reuters*, May 14, 2008.
[94] "Bangladesh-Population," *Encyclopedia of the Nations*, http://www.nationsencyclopedia.com.
[95] "Bangladesh," *CIA World Factbook*, 2010.
[96] Mohammad Mabud, "Bangladesh Population: Prospects and Problems," North South University, Dhaka, December 15, 2008.
[97] "Bangladesh Agriculture: In 21st Century," *Perspective*, http://www.perspectivebd.com.
[98] Mohammad T. Chowdhury, "Sustainability of Accelerated Rice Production in Bangladesh," *Bangladesh Journal of Agricultural Research*, September 2009.
[99] "Bangladesh Workers Riot Over Soaring Food Prices," Agence France Presse, April 12, 2008.
[100] "Is Growth in Bangladesh's Rice Production Sustainable?" http://ideas.repec.org.
[101] "Asian States Feel the Pinch," BBC News, April 11, 2008.
[102] "Island Claimed by India and Bangladesh Sinks Below the Waves," *The Guardian*, March 24, 2010.
[103] H. Franchineau, "Bangladesh Fears Climate Change Will Swallow a Third of its Land," *The Washington Times*, September 18, 2009.
[104] "Population Density by Country," http://www.nationmaster.com.

In: Bangladesh and Burma: Background and Issues ISBN: 978-1-61761-219-0
Editor: Brandon E. Stromberg © 2011 Nova Science Publishers, Inc.

Chapter 2

BANGLADESH: BACKGROUND AND UNITED STATES RELATIONS

Bruce Vaughn

SUMMARY

Bangladesh (the former East Pakistan) gained its independence in 1971, following India's intervention in a rebellion against West Pakistan (currently called Pakistan). Democratic elections in 1991 ended two decades of authoritarian rule in Dhaka. The Bangladesh National Party (BNP), which led the ruling coalition of the previous government, and the leading opposition party, the Awami League (AL), traditionally have dominated Bangladeshi politics. The BNP is led by former Prime Minister Khaleda Zia while the AL is led by Sheikh Hasina. Bangladesh has been a largely moderate and democratic majority Muslim country. This status has been under threat from a combination of political violence, weak governance, poverty, corruption, and Islamist militancy. When in opposition, both parties have sought to regain control of the government through demonstrations, labor strikes, and transport blockades.

Bangladesh is now ruled by a military-backed caretaker government led by Fakhruddin Ahmed that appears unlikely to relinquish power in the near term. It is pursuing an anti-corruption drive that could overturn the normal political elites. It is also seeking to put in place voter reforms, including issuing identity cards, and has moved against militant Islamists. While there has been concern that the new military- backed caretaker government would be reluctant to relinquish power, it has presented a roadmap for new elections and a return to democracy in Bangladesh.

Bangladesh is one of the poorest and most corrupt countries of the world. The largely agricultural economy suffers frequent and serious setbacks from cyclones and floods. While economic progress has been made, it has been impaired by rivalry between the two largest political parties. Bangladesh is thought to have large reserves of natural gas.

Political violence has become part of the political landscape in Bangladesh. A.M.S. Kibria, a finance minister in a previous Awami League government, and four others were killed in a bomb attack that also injured 70 at a political rally of the Awami League on January 27, 2005. On August 21, 2004, an apparent political assassination attempt on opposition leader Sheikh Hasina at a political rally in Dhaka killed 22. These two attacks, and widespread bombings on August 17, 2005, that claimed 26 lives and injured dozens others, are the most notable incidents among many in recent years.

U.S. policy toward Bangladesh emphasizes support for political stability and democracy; development; and human rights. The United States has long-standing supportive relations with Bangladesh and has viewed Bangladesh as a moderate voice in the Islamic world. Some analysts are concerned that Islamist parties have gained influence through the political process and that this has created space for militant activities inside the country. Some allege that the presence in the former ruling Bangladesh National Party (BNP) coalition government of two Islamist parties, the Islamiya Okiyya Jote (IOJ) and the Jamaat-e-Islami, contributed to the expansion of Islamist influence in Bangladesh.

RECENT DEVELOPMENTS

Emergency rule by a military-backed caretaker government, currently headed by Fakhruddin Ahmed, is likely to continue through 2007 and into 2008. Under a unique set of rules, the government in Bangladesh is to hand over power to a caretaker government in the months immediately preceding national elections. The Bangladesh National Party did this in 2006 in the lead up to the scheduled January 2007 election. The current political situation came about after emergency rule was declared by President Iajuddin Ahmed following protests and strikes by opposition parties in the lead up to the January 2007 elections. This led to the installation of the present military-backed caretaker government.

The Awami League (AL), which was in opposition to the previous Bangladesh National Party (BNP) government, protested irregularities in the voter list in the lead up to the election that was scheduled for January 2007. These irregularities were independently confirmed by the National Democratic Institute (NDI):

> The [NDI] delegation is deeply concerned that the new Voters' List runs to over 93 million names, a size that is substantially inconsistent with the 2001 census data. A Voters' List containing two-thirds of the population strains credibility ... on the basis of the 2001 Census, the voting age population was approximately 80 million people.[1]

The current military-backed caretaker government has stated that it wishes to hold elections in 2008 after implementing electoral reforms to include a new voter list and improved voter identification. Observers believe that the military has been reluctant to play a more direct role for fear of jeopardizing its lucrative international peacekeeping work.[2] Some observers are already concerned that elections may be further delayed. According to Brad Adams, Asia Director for Human Rights Watch, the army is running the country and does not intend to relinquish power in the near future. It has been reported that as many as 200,000 people, including leading politicians, have been jailed under the emergency.[3]

Disillusionment among Bangladeshis with the two traditional ruling political parties, the Awami League led by Sheikh Hasina and the Bangladesh National Party led by Khaleda Zia, meant that emergency rule has been broadly welcomed by the populace. Zia was prime minister from 1991 to 1996 and from 2001 to 2006, while Hasina was prime minister from 1996 to 2001. There are reportedly signs that discontent may emerge should elections be indefinitely delayed. Bangladesh's economy is projected to grow by approximately 6% through 2008 despite the political turmoil.[4]

Zia, Hasina, Ershad and the Future Political Landscape

Under its anti-corruption drive the caretaker government has moved decisively against the established political parties. This has the potential to fundamentally change the political landscape of Bangladesh. Bangladesh has for many years been one of the world's most corrupt nations. Charges have now been brought against both AL leader Hasina as well as Zia of the BNP. Hasina was arrested on charges of extortion while Zia was charged with tax evasion on July 16, 2007. Hussein Muhamad Ershad of the Jatiya Party has also recently retired from politics. Some observers question the caretaker government's motives and commitment to restore democracy in Bangladesh in light of these moves.[5] In recent commentary in the *Daily Star* of Bangladesh it has been asserted that "... it now seems clearer than ever that the oligopoly of the existing political parties is what the current administration is intent on breaking up." Concern has also been raised that the caretaker government may have unintentionally created a vacuum through its anti-corruption assault on the established parties that the relatively unscathed Islamist parties may be well positioned to fill.[6]

The Election Commission is moving forward with voter identity cards that reportedly will include photographs of each individual. This is a process that is thought will take at least a year to implement in Bangladesh, a nation with 147 million people and high illiteracy. Restrictions on political assembly remain in force in Bangladesh. Many have hoped that the state of emergency could begin to be lifted. Allowing indoor political meetings would be one way to initiate a lifting of the state of emergency.

The Islamists

The roughly even split in support for the AL and the BNP has given small Islamist parties, some of which have ties to violent Islamist radicals, a disproportionate voice in Bangladesh's government and politics in recent years. Islamists support the imposition of Sharia law in Bangladesh. While Islam has served as a legitimizing political force in Bangladesh, which is 88% Muslim, the present military-backed caretaker government has emphasized anti-corruption as a legitimizing concept and has demonstrated its resolve to fight radical Islamists. This has included the execution of previously captured violent extremist leaders. The country's two main Islamist militant groups are the Jamaat-ul-Mujahideen and the Jagrata Muslim Janata Bangladesh (JMJB), both of which were outlawed under the previous BNP government.[7]

Army forces captured Habibur Rahman Bulbuli in June 2007. Bulbuli was leader of the Khelafat Majlish that is a component of the Islamiya Okiya Jote, which was a junior partner in the former BNP government of Khaleda Zia.

Bulbuli has claimed to be a veteran of fighting in Afghanistan and a follower of Osama bin Laden.[8] In June 2007, Bangladesh police charged Mufti Hannan and three accomplices, who are all now in prison, with trying to assassinate the British High Commissioner Anwar Choudhury in 2004. Choudhury, who is of Bangladeshi origin, was wounded in a grenade attack as were some 50 others. Three were also killed in the attack which occurred at a shrine near Choudhury's ancestral home.[9] The Rapid Action Battalion (RAB) reportedly captured four suspected members of Jamaat-ul-Mujahideen, as well as grenades and explosives, near Kishoregani northwest of Dhaka on July 18, 2007.[10] A United Nations Counter Terror Assessment Team traveled to Bangladesh in June 2007. It will reportedly make recommendations on what technical assistance is needed by Bangladesh.[11]

Political Context

The intense and at times violent political rivalry between the country's two main political parties, the Bangladesh National Party (BNP) and the Awami League (AL), and the presence of radical Islamist parties and groups, have defined Bangladesh's poor political environment in recent years. Other challenges facing Bangladesh include rampant corruption, dysfunctional parliamentary government, a weak judiciary, poor human rights, communal conflict, periodic environmental disasters, and poverty.[12]

An understanding of the close political balance between the two main parties in the last election is necessary to understand the political maneuvering that has taken place in the lead-up to the elections that were scheduled for January 22, 2007. Bangladesh has a 300 seat unicameral national parliament known as the Jatiya Sangsad. During the last election, held on October 1, 2001, the Bangladesh National Party (BNP), led by Prime Minister Khaleda Zia, and its alliance partners won 41% of votes. The BNP's alliance partners in that election included the Jamaat-e-Islami (JI), the Islamiya Okiya Jote (IOJ) and the Jatiya Party (JP) - Manzur Faction. They were opposed by the Awami League, led by Sheikh Hasina, which won 40% of the vote. The number of seats won by party were as follows: BNP: 193, AL: 58, JI: 17, JP (Ershad Faction): 14, IOJ: 2, JP (Manzur Faction): 4, and others: 12.[13]

Elections in Bangladesh are to be held every five years. Bangladesh has instituted a provision for the President to appoint an interim government in the immediate lead-up to polls in order to prevent the incumbent government from using the powers of office to unfair political advantage. The United Kingdom

Parliamentary Human Rights Group reported in October 2006 that prospects for a free and fair election in Bangladesh looked "bleak." Others have agreed with this assessment. Manipulation of voters lists, rampant and escalating political violence, the assassination of former finance Minister Shah AMS Kibria, the attempt on the British High Commissioner's life, grenade attacks against AL leader Hasina, the suicide bombing of two judges, the simultaneous bombings across the country in August 2005, and killings by the elite Rapid Action Battalion have been identified as sources of instability and reasons for pessimism on the democratic process in Bangladesh.[14]

Former Prime Minister Sheik Hasina of the Awami League heads an alliance that sought to wrest power from the former BNP government headed by Khaleda Zia. Hasina and the Awami League alliance threatened to boycott the January 22 elections. The Awami league held large scale demonstrations in December 2006 to highlight their demands, which included a revision of the voter list.[15]

The traditionally more secular of the two main political parties, the Awami League, reportedly signed an agreement with the Khelafat Majlis, considered by some to be a pro-Taliban style Islamist group, in the lead-up to the polls scheduled for January 2007.[16] Former General Hussein Muhamad Ershad, who ruled Bangladesh from 1982 to 1990, had joined the AL to contest the election but was deemed a fugitive of justice by the government after fleeing corruption charges.[17] Some had viewed Ershad as a possible kingmaker, or, in the case of Bangladesh, a queenmaker, in the scheduled but postponed polls of January 2007.

Former U.S. Ambassador Patricia Butenis stated that Bangladeshis "have suffered because the political parties ... could not agree on the basic rules of the game ... the hard part is actually creating political parties that are genuinely democratic in practice and outlook, parties that focus on issues and the national interest instead of personalities...."[18]

In the lead-up to the scheduled January 2007 election, observers generally feared that political infighting, corruption, rising Islamist extremism, and political violence would further erode the Bangladesh government's ability to effectively or democratically govern. Bombings and other violence "targeted opponents of Islamization: secular and leftist politicians, intellectuals and journalist, and religious minority groups."[19] Bangladesh's status as a secular and moderate state, as well as its democratic process, has been jeopardized as a result of the approach taken by the two main political parties. Further, there is concern that should Bangladesh become a failed state, or a state with increased influence by Islamist extremists, it could increasingly serve as a base of operations for terrorist activity.[20]

U.S.-BANGLADESH RELATIONS

Deputy Assistant Secretary of State for South and Central Asia John Gastright stated in testimony before the House Subcommittee on the Middle East and South Asia on August 1, 2007, that Bangladesh was "... fast becoming a democracy in name only, where money, cronyism and intimidation increasingly dictated the outcome of elections." In discussing the shift to the new military-backed caretaker government, he stated that U.S. was initially "troubled that this dramatic shift in government might signal a hidden agenda to indefinitely delay a return to democracy and conceal a secret military coup." He added that the caretaker government was responsive to calls for outlining a roadmap to elections and the restoration of democracy.[21]

The United States has long-standing supportive relations with Bangladesh and has viewed Bangladesh as a moderate voice in the Islamic world. Major U.S. interests in Bangladesh include political stability and democratization; continuation of economic reform and market-opening policies; social and economic development; environmental issues; counterterrorism; and improvement of the human rights situation. Many in the United States would particularly like to bolster Bangladesh's democracy, which is destabilized by political violence. In early 2003, Dhaka was the site of modestly-sized street demonstrations in opposition to the U.S.-led invasion of Iraq.[22]

Bangladesh is a recipient of significant international aid. It has received more than $30 billion from foreign donors since its independence in 1971. The State Department has requested a total of $88,790,000 in assistance for Bangladesh in the FY2008 budget request.[23] U.S. assistance to Bangladesh supports health and economic development programs, the improvement of working conditions, including the elimination of child labor. P.L. 480 funds provide food assistance for the poorest families and for disaster relief. International Military Education and Training programs strengthen the international peacekeeping force of Bangladesh, which is a leading contributor of U.N. peacekeeping personnel.

The United States is Bangladesh's largest export destination. Bangladesh's main import partners are India, China, Kuwait, Singapore, Japan, and Hong Kong.[24] The United States exports wheat, fertilizer, cotton, communications equipment, and medical supplies, among other goods to Bangladesh. Ready made garments and jute carpet backing are two of Bangladesh's key exports to the U.S. The United States has generally had a negative balance of trade with Bangladesh since 1986.[25]

U.S. Assistance to Bangladesh, 2003-2007 (thousands of dollars)

Account	FY2003	FY2004	FY2005	FY2006	FY2007[c]	FY2008 req.
CSH	27,600	35,500	33,412	31,509	—	39,615
DA	21,391	18,200	16,535	10,889	—	39,650
ESF	4,000	4,971	4,960	4,950	—	0
FMF	0	0	248	990	—	875
IMET	772	862	1,035	930	—	800
INCLE	0	0	0	0	—	1,500
NADR	0	0	893	5,094	—	6,350
Peace Corps	1,248	1,566	1,773	706	—	0
Totals	55,011	61,099	58,856	55,068	—	88,790
Food Aid						
P.L. 480 Title II Grant[a]	38,577	33,451	22,122	30,207	—	31,000
Section 416(b)[b]	49	53	3,257	3,833	—	—

Sources: CRS Report RL3 1362, *U.S. Foreign Aid to East and Southeast Asia*, by Thomas Lum. U.S. Department of State, USAID, U.S. Department of Agriculture.

Note: Child Survival and Health (CSH), Development Assistance (DA), Economic Support Funds (ESF), Foreign Military Financing (FMF), International Military Education and Training, (IMET), Non-proliferation, Anti-terrorism, Demining and Related programs (NADR).

a. USAID data — includes freight costs.
b. USDA data — does not include freight costs.
c. Support is expected to be close to FY2006 levels.

GOVERNMENT AND POLITICS

Formerly known as East Pakistan, and before that as the East Bengal region of British India, Bangladesh gained its independence from Pakistan following a civil war in December 1971. The country's topography consists mainly of low lying alluvial plain, which is drained by some 700 rivers joining to form five major river systems that flow into the Bay of Bengal. The densely populated country is subject to the annual ravages of cyclones and flooding. There is a very real possibility that global warming may lead to rising sea levels that would likely flood much of Bangladesh's low-lying costal areas.

Following two decades of authoritarian rule, Bangladesh held its first democratic elections in 1991. Since then, Dhaka's politics have been characterized by a bitter struggle between the Bangladesh National Party (BNP) and the Awami League (AL), and particularly between the two leaders of the respective parties, Prime Minister Khaleda Zia (1991-1996, 2001-present) and former Prime Minister Sheikh Hasina Wajed (1996-2001). Zia is the widow of former president and military strongman Ziaur Rahman, who was assassinated in 1981. Sheikh Hasina is the daughter of Bangladeshi independence leader and first prime minister Sheikh Mujibur Rahman, who was assassinated in 1975. Both the AL and the BNP, when out of power, have devoted their energies to parliamentary boycotts, demonstrations, and strikes in an effort to unseat the ruling party. The strikes often succeed in immobilizing the government and disrupting economic activity. The President's powers are largely ceremonial, though they are expanded during the tenure of a caretaker government.

BANGLADESH IN BRIEF

Population: 150.448 million
growth rate: 2.06%
Area: 147,570 sq. km. (slightly smaller than Iowa)
Capital: Dhaka
Ethnic Groups: Bengali 98%; tribal less than 1 million
Language: Bengali (official); English widely used
Religion: Muslim 83%; Hindu 16%
Life Expectancy at Birth: 62.84
Infant Mortality: 59.12 per 1,000 births
Inflation: 7.2%
Unemployment: 2.5%
Gross Domestic Product: *6.6% growth with per capita ppp* = $2,300
Labor Force: Agriculture 63%, Industry 11%, and Services 26%
Key Exports: Garments, jute, leather, frozen fish, seafood

> **Key Export Partners:** U.S. 25%, Germany 12.7%, U.K. 9.9%, France 5%
>
> Sources: CIA World Factbook; Reuters; U.S. Departments of State and Commerce; World Bank.

The BNP and its alliance partners were elected in October 2001. Observers declared the poll generally free and fair, though more than 100 people were killed in pre-election violence. The AL, however, claimed that the elections were rigged and boycotted parliament for several months in protest. Since June 2002, the AL regularly has boycotted most parliamentary sessions or walked out of sessions in protest. The BNP has published a white paper on the misuse of power, mismanagement and corruption allegedly committed during the period of AL rule. There has been some concern about the former BNP ruling coalition's inclusion of the fundamentalist Jamaat-e-Islami party, which supports turning secular and moderate Bangladesh into an Islamic republic.[26]

There has been much political violence in Bangladesh in recent years. In January 2005 the State Department issued a statement that "strongly condemned" the bomb attack that killed four, including former Awami League Finance Minister A.M.S. Kibria, and injured 70 at a political rally of the Awami League on January 27, 2005. The incident was described by the State Department as "the latest in a series of often deadly attacks on prominent leaders of the political opposition and civil society." On August 21, 2004, grenades were hurled in an apparent political assassination attempt on opposition leader Sheikh Hasina at a political rally in Dhaka and killed 22. These two attacks, and widespread bombings on August 17, 2005 marked a rising tide of political violence in Bangladesh. The formerly ruling Awami League alleged that the Jamaat-e-Islami and Islamiya Okiyya Jote parties protected the radicals responsible for the violence from prosecution by the government.[27]

Corruption

Corruption is widespread in Bangladesh. Berlin-based Transparency International ranked Bangladesh as among the world's most corrupt countries.[28] The Index of Economic Freedom has ranked Bangladesh's economy as "mostly unfree" and states that "...corruption also serves as a nontariff barrier."[29] According to one source, Bangladesh took disciplinary action against a significant percentage of its police force in recent years for offenses ranging from corruption to dereliction of duty.[30] According to one source, Bangladesh's largest port, Chittagong, which handles 90% of all trade to Bangladesh, is hampered by widespread corruption and a rapid increase in piracy.[31] U.S. Assistant Secretary of State for South Asia Richard Boucher has stated "the main obstacles [for Bangladesh] are corruption and poor governance."[32]

TERRORISM AND ISLAMIST EXTREMISM IN BANGLADESH[33]

Political Ties to Terrorist Organizations

There are several terrorist and militant extremist groups operating in Bangladesh including Harkat ul Jihad al Islami (HuJi), Jagrata Muslim Janata Bangladesh (JMJB), and Jama'atul Mujahideen Bangladesh (JMB). Bangladeshi opposition, analysts, and media observers have alleged that the presence in the former ruling Bangladesh National Party (BNP) Coalition government of two Islamist parties, the Islamiya Okiyya Jote (IOJ) and the Jamaat-e-Islami, had expanded Islamist influence in Bangladesh and created space within which terrorist and extremist groups could operate. Islami Okiyya Jote is thought to have ties to the radical Harkat-ul-Jihad-alIslami (HuJI).[34] Jamaat also reportedly has ties to Harkat ul-Jihad-i-Islami which has ties to Al Qaeda. Harkat leader Fazlul Rahman signed an Osama bin Laden holy war declaration in 1998.[35] JMB seeks the imposition of Sharia law for Bangladesh and is thought responsible for the widespread and coordinated August 2005 bombings. HuJI has been implicated in the January 2002 attack on the American Center in Calcutta, India.[36] HuJI, or the Movement of Islamic Holy War, is on the U.S. State Department's list of "other terrorist organizations," has links to Pakistani militant groups, and has a cadre strength of several thousand.[37] Awami League sources claimed that fundamentalist leader Bangla Bhai had ties to Jamaat-e-Islami.[38] AL leader Sheikh Hasina has accused the government of "letting loose communal extremist forces."[39] Some news sources have reported that international extremists are using Bangladeshi passports and that some are obtaining them with the assistance of sympathetic officials at various Bangladesh Embassies.[40]

Two senior members of IOJ have reportedly been connected with the reemergence of Harkat ul Jihad (HuJi) under the name "Conscious Islamic People."[41] It has also been reported that the political wing of HuJi will seek to enter politics under the name Islami Gono Andolon.[42] The former BNP government had denied the presence of significant terrorist elements in the country and reportedly had even expelled BNP lawmaker Abu Hena from the BNP for speaking out against extremist activities at a time when the official view was that such extremists did not exist.[43]

The former BNP government eventually moved to suppress the Jamaat-ul-Mujahideen (JMB) and the Jagrata Muslim Janata Bangladesh (JMJB) terrorist groups in Bangladesh. The government sentenced to death JMB leaders Shaikh Abdur Rahman and Siddiq ul Islam, also known as "Bangla Bhai,"as well as five other JMB members, in May 2006. They were subsequently executed for their role in the bombings.[44] The two Islamist militant leaders received their sentences for the murder of two judges in November of 2005. They are also thought to have been behind widespread bombings in Bangladesh and to have sought to replace the secular legal system with Sharia law through such attacks. The government also reportedly has arrested some 900 lower-level militants, seven known senior leaders, four out of 11 commanders, and some 20 district leaders on terrorism charges.[45] Despite this, the opposition Awami League (AL) party Leader Sheikh Hassina stated "militants are partners of the government ... the government catches a few militants whenever foreign guests visit Bangladesh." She has also alleged that Jamaat has 15,000 guerillas and its own training camps. Hassina has also stated that the arrest of JMB operatives is "only the tip of the iceberg."[46]

It appears that the government shifted its position on the necessity of acknowledging and addressing Islamist militants in August of 2005. In response, JMB leader Rahman reportedly has stated, "masks will fall and you [implying the authorities] will be exposed." Such an allegation is consistent with allegations by the AL opposition, which has accused the government, or more likely elements within the government, of allowing Islamist militancy to rise in Bangladesh.[47]

Selig Harrison, a prominent South Asian Analyst, noted in early August 2006 that "a growing Islamic fundamentalist movement linked to al-Qaeda and Pakistani intelligence agencies is steadily converting the strategically located nation of Bangladesh into a new regional hub for terrorist operations that reach into India and Southeast Asia." Harrison points out that former Prime Minister Khaleda Zia's Bangladesh National Party's coalition alliance with the Jamaat-e-Islami Party of Bangladesh led to a "Faustian bargain" that brought Jamaat officials into the government. These officials, he argued, in turn have allowed Taliban-styled squads to operate with increasing impunity. Jamaat's entry into the former BNP government also reportedly led to fundamentalist control over large parts of the Bangladesh economy, Islamist Madrassa schools that act as fronts for terrorist activity, fundamentalist inroads into the armed forces, and rigging (by manipulating voter lists) of the elections that were originally scheduled for January 2007.[48]

The State Department continues to view the government of Bangladesh as working to thwart terrorist activities. In responding to a question from an Indian journalist who asserted that Bangladesh "is not only aiding and abetting the separatist Indian guerilla forces, but is also ... supporting and helping the Islamic forces to fight against India," Assistant Secretary of State for South and Central Asian Affairs Richard Boucher stated the following:

> We see that Bangladesh is a very populated country with a developing security service, a developing ability to fight terrorism, with some successes already that they can show in terms of arresting the leaders of the major terrorist group that has been operating in Bangladesh, but with a lot of work left to do, in terms of getting the whole network and getting, stopping other people who might be operating there.[49]

He also stated that the U.S. government was following the situation in Bangladesh "closely."[50]

Bangladesh's Connection to Bombings in India

On July 11, 2006, a series of coordinated bomb blasts killed approximately 200 persons while wounding some 500 others on commuter trains in Bombay (Mumbai), India. Indian authorities subsequently arrested several individuals reportedly with ties to terrorist groups in Bangladesh and Nepal who were "directly or indirectly" linked to Pakistan. Indian intelligence officials have portrayed the bombers as being backed by Pakistan-supported terrorist groups. Pakistan has denied these allegations.[51] Allegations had been made that the explosives had come from Bangladesh. In response, Bangladesh authorities stated that the Jamaat ul-Mujahideen (JMB) attacks in Bangladesh on August 17, 2005, which killed 30 in a series of nationwide blasts, were of Indian origin.[52] Six of the eight arrested in India in connection with the bombings are thought to have received training from Lashkar-e-Toiba at terrorist camps in Pakistan. Lashkar is a Pakistan-based militant terrorist group.

While most of the focus in India has been on Pakistan, Bharatiya Janata Party (BJP) President Rajnath Singh has called on the Indian government to pressure Bangladesh to dismantle terrorist training centers in Bangladesh. The BJP is the leading opposition party in India. Singh also stated that Bangladesh had become "a centre of Islamic fundamentalist forces."[53] The anti-terrorism squad investigating the Bombay blasts also interrogated a number of individuals in a village in Tripura, India, that borders Bangladesh.[54] A bombing in Varanasi, India, in March 2006 also reportedly had links to HuJi in Bangladesh.[55]

ECONOMICS, TRADE, AND DEVELOPMENT

Bangladesh is one of the poorest and most densely populated countries in the world. The annual per capita income is about $2,300 in purchasing power parity. The agricultural sector employs approximately 63% of the workforce and accounts for 19.9% of GDP while industry employs 11% and contributes 20.6% of GDP.[56] Services account for 26% of the labor force and 59.5% of GDP. The major crop is rice, in which Bangladesh is nearly self-sufficient. Industry is centered mainly on cotton textiles, jute manufacturing, and food processing. Ready-made garments and knitwear are important exports for Bangladesh. Foreign exchange earnings from remittances by Bangladeshis working abroad is another key source of wealth for Bangladesh.[57]

Though Bangladesh is one of the world's poorest countries, its economy has made some progress in recent years. The Bangladeshi economy had, like that of its South Asian neighbors, suffered from years of stagnation under public sector dominance and bureaucratic inefficiency. In 1991, however, Zia's BNP government embarked on an economic reform program aimed at promoting budget discipline and export-led growth. Significant progress was made in reducing the budget deficit, increasing foreign reserves, and attracting new foreign investment. Sheik Hasina's AL government (1996-2001) continued to pursue economic reforms, making some headway in improving the investment climate. However, bureaucratic delays and labor union resistance have hindered implementation of many reforms, including major privatization efforts. Moreover, crippling strikes led by both major political parties when out of power have resulted in a loss of foreign investor confidence. The Bangladeshi economy has been described as "mostly unfree,"as a result of high levels of trade protectionism and regulation, and an extensive black market economy.[58] Bangladesh has been a pioneer in the field of micro enterprise lending programs.

Former Prime Minister Zia called for "faster and deeper economic integration" for the member states of the South Asian Association of Regional Cooperation (SAARC).[59] SAARC considered a Free Trade Agreement for member states at a meeting held in Dhaka. The United States was recently given observer status at SAARC. SAARC granted such status to China and Japan in 2005.[60]

ENVIRONMENTAL ISSUES

Frequent and disastrous floods take a heavy toll on lives, homes, crops, and livestock in Bangladesh. In 1998, Bangladesh suffered its worst flooding of the 20th century. Lasting three months and covering two-thirds of the country, the floods left more than 1,000 dead and 25 million homeless or marooned. The increase of flood devastation in recent years is related to growing population pressure and deforestation in upstream areas of Bangladesh and neighboring India and Nepal. There are reports that Bangladesh has recently improved its disaster management. Another key environmental issue for Bangladesh has been the sharing with India of Ganges (called Padma in Bangladesh) River waters. In the early 1990s, Bangladesh claimed that diversion of the river water to India had increased salinity and desertification of downstream soils and contributed to increased flooding in Bangladesh. In 1996, Bangladesh and India signed a 30-year agreement that settled the issue by giving Bangladesh a share of the river waters for the first time since 1988, when a previous agreement expired. Nonetheless, major water management issues — including hydroelectric power, deforestation, and water storage — remain to be addressed on a region-wide basis. A serious environmental problem that has arisen in recent years is the dangerous levels of naturally occurring arsenic found in drinking water being supplied to millions of Bangladeshis through a vast system of tubewells that tap the arsenic-contaminated ground water.[61]

HUMAN RIGHTS AND RELIGIOUS FREEDOM

According to the Department of State's *Country Reports on Human Rights Practices*, the Bangladesh "government's human rights record remained poor, and the government continued to commit numerous serious abuses."

> ... extrajudicial killings, arbitrary arrest and detention, and politically motivated violence were among the most egregious violations. Security forces acted with impunity, and committed acts of physical and psychological torture. In addition violence against journalists continued, as did infringement on religious freedoms. Government corruption remained a significant problem. Violence against women and children also was a major problem, as was trafficking in persons. [62]

Human Rights Watch found in 2006 that the BNP government had "aligned itself with extremist groups that foment violence against the minority Ahmadiyya community." Ahmadiyyas are a self identified Islamic community that differs with mainstream Islam on whether the prophet Mohammad is the final prophet. BNP government coalition partners JI and the IOJ do not recognize Ahmadiayys as Muslims "and have been involved in fomenting religious violence against them and other religious minorities."[63] The government has also been accused of failing to prosecute attacks against journalists by supporters of the BNP.

Bangladesh's elite anti-crime and anti-terrorist RAB is thought to be responsible for killing at least 350 people in custody and for the torture of hundreds of others.[64]

The government's failure to punish RAB members for unlawful killings and torture is viewed as indicative of consent for RAB actions. The RAB was created in 2004 and is known to torture by boring holes in suspects with electric drills as well as using electric shock and beatings. The RAB has attributed deaths associated with its operations as the result of crossfire.[65]

The case of Bangladesh Weekly Blitz editor Salah Uddin Shoaib Choudhury highlights how the rise of Islamist tendencies have undermined Bangladesh's image as a tolerant Muslim state. The BNP government brought charges against Choudhury stating that

> By praising the Jews and the Christians, by attempting to travel to Israel and by predicting the so-called rise of Islamist militancy in the country and expressing such thoughts in writing inside the country and abroad, you have

tried to damage the image and relations of Bangladesh with the outside world. For which, charges ... are brought against you.

After 17 months in prison Choudhury was released, though his offices were bombed and the government continues to press the charges against him. Choudhury could be hanged if convicted. The media has reported that the efforts of U.S. Representatives Mark Kirk played a role in Choudhury's release. Kirk was joined by 18 cosponsors when he introduced legislation calling for the charges against Choudhury to be dropped.[66]

FOREIGN RELATIONS

Relations between New Delhi and Dhaka have been strained in recent years as Indian officials have accused Bangladesh of harboring both agents of Pakistan's intelligence service and separatist militants fighting the New Delhi government in India's northeastern states, such as the All Tripura Tiger Force.[67] Dhaka has denied the accusations as "totally baseless and irresponsible." Acrimony over migration issues led to periodic and lethal exchanges of gunfire between the border security forces of Bangladesh and India.[68] Bangladesh reportedly refused a request by India to have transit rights across Bangladesh to link with its northeastern states. With the exception of a small corridor, Bangladesh separates India from its northeastern states.

Border incidents, including exchanges of small arms fire between Indian Border Security Force and Bangladesh Rifles soldiers, continue to be an irritant in India- Bangladesh relations. India is building a fence along the 4,000 kilometer border with Bangladesh to stem the flow of illegal immigrants. India has also demanded that Bangladesh suppress separatist militants that cross the border. India has alleged that there are some 172 insurgent bases in Bangladesh. Bangladesh has denied their existence.[69]

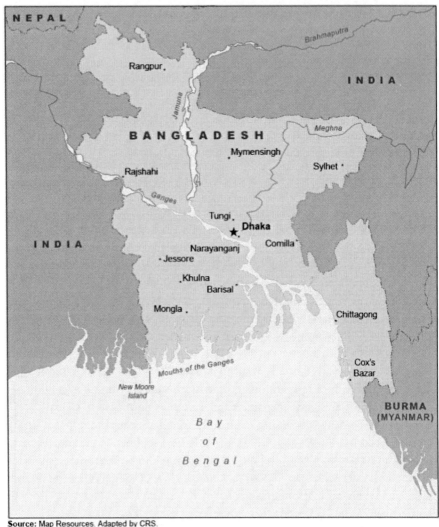

Source: Map Resources. Adapted by CRS.

Figure 1. Map of Bangladesh

Bangladesh is strategically situated between South and Southeast Asia and is located in proximity to both India and China. Bangladesh's natural gas deposits, estimated at between 32 trillion and 80 trillion cubic feet,[70] increase Bangladesh's strategic importance to India and China, which may seek to secure additional energy resources for future economic growth. Arguments in Bangladesh against developing the gas reserves for export have focused on the need to secure a 50-year supply of domestic energy requirements before entering the export market. It has been estimated that Bangladesh's energy needs to 2050 would require 63 trillion cubic feet of gas.[71] Bangladesh and China signed a Defense Co-operation Agreement in December 2002.[72]

End Notes

[1] "Report of the National Democratic Institute (NDI) Pre-election Delegation to Bangladesh's 2006/2007 Parliamentary Elections," *National Democratic Institute*, Dhaka, September 11, 2006.
[2] "Bangladesh in the Balance," *CSIS South Asia Monitor*, August 1, 2007.
[3] Yaroslav Trofimov, "How Army's Coup Stalled Democracy in Bangladesh, — U.S., U.N. Backed Move Ahead of Vote," *The Wall Street Journal*, June 5, 2007.
[4] "Bangladesh Country Report," *The Economist Intelligence Unit*, June 2007.
[5] Lisa Curtis, "Protecting Democracy in Bangladesh," *The Heritage Foundation*, July 17, 2007.
[6] Zafar Sobhan "Three Down, One to Go," *The Daily Star*, July 6, 2007 as reprinted in "Bangladesh Paper Warns Government Against Role of Islamists in Future Politics," *BBC News*, July 7, 2007.
[7] "B'desh Police Say Find No Trace of "New" al-Qaeda," *Reuters*, May 20, 2007.
[8] "Bangladesh Forces Capture Afghan War Veteran Bulbuli," *Asia News International*, May 16, 2007.
[9] B'desh Charges Islamists for Attacks on U.K. Envoy," *Reuters*, June 9, 2007.
[10] "Bangladesh Arrests Islamists, Seizes Explosives," *Reuters*, July 18, 2007.
[11] Masud Karim, "UN Team to Help Bangladesh Tackle Terrorism," *Reuters*, June 3, 2007.
[12] "Bangladesh Today," *International Crisis Group*, October 23, 2006.
[13] Bangladesh elects its representatives by district. CIA World Factbook, [http://www.cis.gov/cia/publications/factbook/geos/bg].
[14] "Prospect for Free, Fair Election in Bangladesh "Bleak" - UK Parliamentary Group," *BBC News*, October 2, 2006.
[15] Parveen Ahmed, "Bangladesh Political Alliance threatens More Protests of Upcoming Election," *Associated Press*, December 18, 2006.
[16] "Hasina Deal with Bangladesh Islamists Sparks Criticism," *Reuters*, December 26, 2006.
[17] "Bangladesh Ex-Military Ruler Asked to Surrender," *Agence France Presse*, December 26, 2006.
[18] Ambassador Patricia Butenis, "Elections The Road Ahead," Dhaka University, December 17, 2006.
[19] Stephen Ulph, "Nationwide Bombing Campaign in Bangladesh," *The Jamestown Foundation*, August 19, 2005.
[20] Many in Bangladesh have not wanted to develop Bangladesh gas resources for export to India. "Bangladesh: Country Risk Overview," *Global Insight*, May 2006.
[21] Statement of John Gastright Deputy Assistant Secretary of State for South and Central Asian Affairs Before the House Committee on Foreign Affairs, Subcommittee on the Middle East and South Asia, August 1, 2007.
[22] "Text: Powell, Bangladesh Foreign Minister Khan Confer in Washington Jan 24," USIS Washington File, January 24, 2003; "Bangladesh Port City Sees Largest Anti-War Protest," *Reuters News*, April 6, 2003.
[23] "South and Central Asia," *Budget Justification Document for 2007*, Department of State, 2006, p. 494.
[24] "Bangladesh," *CIA World Factbook*, August 8, 2006.
[25] "Background Notes: Bangladesh," U.S. Department of State, August, 2005.

[26] "Foreign Observers Say Bangladesh Vote Was Fair," Reuters News, October 2, 2001; "Zia's Victory," *Asiaweek*, October 12, 2001; "New Premier in Bangladesh Vows to Stamp Out Corruption," *New York Times*, October 11, 2001.
[27] Roland Buerk,"Bangladesh and Islamic Militants," *BBC News*, February 25, 2005.
[28] The index ranks 159 countries based on a composite of 16 surveys drawn from 10 institutions gathering the perceptions of business people and analysts. The index defines corruption as the abuse of public office for private gain. (2005 Transparency International Corruption Perceptions Index, [http://www.infoplease.com].)
[29] "Bangladesh," 2006 Index of Economic Freedom, Heritage Foundation, [http://www.heritage.org].
[30] "Bangladesh Punishes Nearly Two Thirds of its Police Force," *Reuters*, August 20, 2006.
[31] Elizabeth Mills, "Anger After Bangladeshi Port is Named Worst for Piracy," *Global Insight*, July 28, 2006.
[32] "Corruption, Intra-party Conflicts Challenge Bangladesh's Next Elections," *United News of Bangladesh*, May 18, 2006.
[33] For a more in-depth discussion of the rise of Islamist fundamentalism and the nexus with terrorist activity in Bangladesh, see Hiranmay Karlekar, *Bangladesh: The Next Afghanistan?* (New Delhi: Sage Publishers, 2005), Sumit Ganguly, "The Rise of Islamist Militancy in Bangladesh," U.S. Institute of Peace Special Report, August 2006 and CRS Report RL32259, *Terrorism in South Asia*, by Alan Kronstadt and Bruce Vaughn.
[34] Roland Buerk, "Bangladesh and Islamic Militants," *BBC News*, February 25, 2005.
[35] "Bangladesh Becoming a Regional Terror Hub," *Hindustan Times*, August 3, 2006.
[36] "Bangladesh's First Suicide Bombers," *Janes Terrorism and Security Monitor*, January 18, 2006.
[37] Office of the Coordinator for Counterterrorism, Department of State, *Patterns of Global Terrorism, 2003,* April 29, 2004.
[38] Roland Buerk, "Bangladesh's Escalating Extremism," *BBC News*, November 29, 2005.
[39] Roland Buerk, "Dhaka Struggles to Respond to Bombs," *BBC News*, August, 2005.
[40] "International Terrorists Using Bangladeshi Passports," *Notes From the Bangla Media*, August 30, 2006, The U.S. Embassy, Dhaka, "Bangladesh Press Selection," *BBC News*, August 30, 2006; and "BSF Wants Anup Chetia Deported," *Indian Express*, August 29, 2006.
[41] "IOJ Behind Reemergence of Harkatul Jihad," Notes From the Bangla Media, United States Embassy, Dhaka, August 22, 2006.
[42] "War on Terror Digest 21-22 Aug 06," *BBC Monitoring*, August 22, 2006.
[43] "Summer of Discontent in the BNP," *United News of Bangladesh*, June 9, 2006.
[44] "Bangladesh Arrests To Senior Leaders of Banned Militant Group," *BBC News*, July 12, 2007.
[45] "Bangladesh Coalition Partners to Face Election Together Amid Terrorism Charges," *Open Source Center*, July 13, 2006.
[46] "Militants Arrest Meant to Impress US: Hassina," *Hindustan Times*, August 4, 2006.
[47] "Bangladesh Blast Masterminds Sentenced to Death," *Agence France Presse*, May 29, 2006.
[48] Selig Harrison, "A New Hub for Terrorism? In Bangladesh, An Islamic Movement with Al-Qaeda Ties is on the Rise," *The Washington Post*, August 2, 2006.
[49] "Richard Boucher Holds a News Conference in Calcutta, India," *CQ Transcripts*, August 4, 2006.
[50] "U.S. Wants Pakistan to Move Against Terrorists," *The Hindu*, August 5, 2006.
[51] "Three Arrested Over Mumbai Bombs Linked to Pakistan," *Financial Times*, August 6, 2006.
[52] Waliur Rahman, "Dhaka Dismisses Mumbai Bomb Claim," *BBC News*, July 15, 2006.
[53] "Uproot Terror Camps From Bangla: BJP," *Hindustan Times*, July 19, 2006.
[54] "Mumbai Police Interrogates Terror Suspects in Tripura," *Hindustan Times*, July 19, 2006.
[55] "Bangla Immigrants the Threat Within," *Times of India*, July 14, 2006.
[56] "Bangladesh," CIA World Factbook, August 2006.
[57] Economic statistics from Global Insight, "Bangladesh: Executive Summary," April 14, 2003; and Economist Intelligence Unit, "Country Outlook: Bangladesh," April 2003.

[58] "World Bank VP Arrives for Talks on Bangladesh Reforms," Agence France-Presse, October 16, 2002; Transparency International, *Corruption Perceptions Index 2002*, August 2002, Heritage Foundation 2003 Index of Economic Freedom, November, 2002.

[59] SAARC members include India, Pakistan, Bangladesh, Sri Lanka, Nepal, Bhutan, and The Maldives.

[60] Parveen Ahmed, "South Asian Foreign Ministers Meet in Bangladesh to Discuss Security, Trade," *Associated Press*, August 1, 2006.

[61] "Contamination of Drinking-Water by Arsenic in Bangladesh: A Public Health Emergency," World Health Organization, available at [http://www.who.org]; "Minister: NGOs Exaggerate Threat of Arsenic Contaminated Water in Bangladesh," Associated Press Newswire, September 12, 2002; "Arsenic May Be Tainting Bangladeshi Crops — Study," Reuters News, December 4, 2002; Khabir Ahmad, "Report Highlights Widespread Arsenic Contamination in Bangladesh," *Lancet* (London), July 14, 2001.

[62] "Bangladesh: Country Reports on Human Rights Practices - 2006," Released by the Bureau of Democracy, Human Rights, and Labor," U.S. Department of State, March 6, 2007.

[63] Human Rights watch, "Bangladesh: Government Fails to Act Against Religious Violence," June 16, 2005.

[64] Human Rights Watch, *Judge, Jury and Executioner: Torture and Extrajudicial Killings by Bangladesh's Elite Security Force*, [http://www.hrw.org]

[65] "Bangladesh: Elite Force Torture, Kills Detainees," December 14, 2006 [http://www.hrw.org]

[66] "I Am Not Guilty," *The Wall Street Journal Asia*, November 16, 2006.

[67] Subir Bhaumik, "Arms Arrests Linked to Indian Rebels," *BBC News*, July 3, 2003.

[68] "Friendly Neighbor, Unfriendly Acts," *Hindu* (Madras), November 23, 2002; "India is Causing Trouble for Bangladesh," *International Herald Tribune*, January 22, 2003; "India's Remarks on Bangladesh Aiding Terrorists Rejected," *Xinhua News Agency*, November 8, 2002.

[69] India, Bangladesh Troops Exchange Border Fire," *Comtex News Network*, August 31, 2006 and "India Urges Bangladesh to Dismantle Alleged Rebel Camps," *Dow Jones Newswire*, August 29, 2006.

[70] "In a Model for Lending in Developing Nations, Bangladesh Bank Relies on Peer Pressure for Collateral," *New York Times*, November 22, 2001; "Bangladesh: A More Prosperous Future?," Center for Strategic and International Studies South Asia Monitor, October 1, 1998; "World Bank Official Says Bangladesh Should Export Gas," *BBC News*, November 23, 2001.

[71] "Bangladesh Energy Might Enhance Clout," *Stratfor*, October 22, 2001.

[72] "Broad Based Defense Deal with China on Agenda," *The Independent*, December 23, 2002.

In: Bangladesh and Burma: Background and Issues ISBN: 978-1-61761-219-0
Editor: Brandon E. Stromberg   © 2011 Nova Science Publishers, Inc.

Chapter 3

BURMA'S 2010 ELECTIONS: IMPLICATIONS OF THE NEW CONSTITUTION AND ELECTION LAW

Michael F. Martin

SUMMARY

On an undisclosed date in 2010, Burma plans to hold its first parliamentary elections in 20 years. The elections are to be held under a new constitution, supposedly approved in a national referendum held in 2008 in the immediate aftermath of the widespread destruction caused by Cyclone Nargis. The official results of the constitutional referendum are widely seen as fraudulent, but despite significant domestic and international opposition, Burma's ruling military junta—the State Peace and Development Council (SPDC)—has insisted on conducting the polls as part of what it calls a path to "disciplined democracy."

On March 9, 2010, the SPDC released five new laws for the pending parliamentary elections. Three of the laws are about the three main types of parliaments stipulated in the constitution—the two houses of the national parliament (*Pyidaungsu Hluttaw*) and the Regional or State parliaments. The fourth law—the Political Parties Registration Law—sets conditions for the registration and operation of political parties in Burma; the fifth law establishes a Union Election Commission to supervise the parliamentary elections and political parties.

The new laws were quickly subjected to sharp criticism, both domestically and overseas. In particular, the law on political parties was widely denounced for placing unreasonable restrictions on the participation of many opposition political leaders and Burma's Buddhist monks and nuns. U.S. Assistant Secretary of State Philip J. Crowley said the Political Parties Registration Law "makes a mockery of the democratic process and ensures that the upcoming elections will be devoid of creditability." There have also been objections to the terms of the Union Election Commission Law and the 17 people subsequently appointed to the commission by the SPDC.

In late September 2009, the Obama Administration adopted a new policy on Burma. The policy keeps most of the elements of the Burma policies of the last two administrations in place, but adds a willingness to engage in direct dialogue with the SPDC on how to promote democracy and human rights in Burma, and greater cooperation on international security issues, such as counternarcotics efforts and nuclear nonproliferation. The Obama Administration accepts that little progress has been made during the seven months that the new policy has been in effect, but has indicated that it will remain in place for now.

There are signs of concern among Members of Congress about the dearth of progress in Burma towards democracy and greater respect for human rights. Nine Senators sent a letter to President Obama on March 26, 2010, urging the imposition of additional economic sanctions on the SPDC in light of "a set of profoundly troubling election laws." However, another Senator perceives "several substantive gestures" on the part of the SPDC, and suggests it is time to increase engagement with the Burmese government.

The 111th Congress has already taken action with respect to Burma, such as renewing the Burmese Freedom and Democracy Act of 2003. If it were to determine that additional actions should be taken, there are several alternatives available. Among those alternatives are holding hearings or seminars on the political situation in Burma, pushing the Obama Administration to implement existing sanctions on Burma more vigorously, and adding or removing existing sanctions.

Overview

On an undisclosed date in 2010, Burma (Myanmar) is to hold its first national parliamentary elections since the ill-fated vote in 1990.[1] Depending on the manner in which the election is held and the outcome of the vote, Burma's prospects for a more democratic government may be at stake. The current ruling military junta—the State Development and Peace Council (SPDC)—is promoting the 2010 election as the fifth step in what it calls a seven-step roadmap to "disciplined democracy." Burma's leading opposition groups are highly skeptical of the SPDC and the 2010 elections, concerned that the SPDC will use a new constitution promulgated in 2008 and legal restrictions placed on participation in the 2010 elections to maintain its stranglehold on power.

Burma's 2010 elections might also pose a challenge to the Obama Administration's policy towards Burma. In September 2009, the U.S. State Department announced a new policy towards Burma, that continued the existing political and economic sanctions, but adding a willingness to engage in high-level discussions with representatives of the SPDC. Previous U.S. administrations had generally refused to participate in high-level discussions with the SPDC.

Burma's two most recent experiences with nation-wide plebiscites do not augur well for the democratization of Burma. In May 1990, the military junta—then known as the State Law and Order Restoration Council (SLORC)—refused to relinquish power when Burma's leading opposition party, the National League for Democracy (NLD), won 392 of the 485 seats in a parliamentary election. In May 2008, the SPDC held a referendum on a new constitution despite the widespread devastation caused by Cyclone Nargis only a few days before the vote.[2] Five days after the referendum, the SPDC announced that over 98% of the eligible voters had cast votes, and that over 92% had voted in favor of the adoption of the constitution—results that were widely viewed as fraudulent.

For the 111th Congress, the 2010 elections may be a strong indicator of the potential for political change in Burma. If, despite political restrictions, the SPDC conducts comparatively free and fair elections with official outcomes that appear to represent the views of the public, there may be calls from the Obama Administration and some sources for Congress to scale back the sanctions. However, if the SPDC manipulates the elections to prevent full participation and/or releases biased or inaccurate results, Congress may choose to increase the political and economic pressure on Burma's ruling military junta.

THE ROAD TO THE 2010 ELECTIONS

The path that has led Burma to the 2010 elections can be traced back to August 30, 2003, when Burma's Prime Minister, General Khin Nyunt, announced the SPDC's seven-step roadmap to democracy (see text box). Between 2004 and 2008, the SPDC progressed through the first three steps of the roadmap, despite significant opposition from various political organizations within Burma and around the world. The adjourned National Convention reconvened in May 2004, after an eight-year break precipitated by an NLD walkout in response to a SPDC crackdown on its political opponents.[3] Despite a continued NLD boycott, the National Convention in September 2007 completed the second step of the roadmap—a draft of the process for transforming Burma into a "disciplined democracy."[4] The SPDC then appointed in October 2007 a special commission to draft the text of a proposed new constitution, based on the work of the National Assembly. In February 2008, the SPDC announced that the drafting of the new constitution was completed. Much of the opposition to the National Convention, its drafting of a new constitution, and the SPDC's "roadmap to democracy," stems from the military's response to the 1990 parliamentary elections.

THE 1990 PARLIAMENTARY ELECTIONS

On May 27, 1990, Burma held national elections to select a new parliament and return the country to civilian rule. After World War II, the former British colony enjoyed a brief period of civilian rule, which was ended by a military coup d'etat in 1958. For the next 30 years, Burma lived under military rule. In the summer of 1988, the people of Burma arose in opposition to the ruling military government, in what is sometimes called the "8888 Uprising." The name refers to the tragic events of August 8, 1988, when soldiers opened fire on the civilian protesters, killing an unknown number of people and started a brutal crackdown on opposition groups and their leaders.

On September 18, 1988, the 19-member State Law and Order Restoration Council (SLORC) assumed power. While their crackdown continued, SLORC announced it did not wish to remain in power for long, and promised to hold multiparty democratic general elections. The date for elections was set for May, 27, 1990.

> ## THE SPDC'S SEVEN-STEP ROADMAP TO DEMOCRACY
>
> (As described by Prime Minister General Khin Nyunt on August 30, 2003)
>
> 1. Reconvene the National Convention (adjourned in 1996)
> 2. Step-by-step implementation of the process necessary for the emergence of a genuine and disciplined democratic system
> 3. Draft a new constitution based on the principles laid out the National Convention
> 4. Adopt the constitution via a national referendum
> 5. Hold free and fair elections to constitute a national legislative assembly based in accordance with the new constitution
> 6. Convene the new national legislative assembly
> 7. Build a modern, developed, and democratic nation

Despite continued suppression and harassment of opposition parties and their candidates, the national vote was held as scheduled. In a surprise to virtually everyone, the leading opposition party, the National League for Democracy, and its leader, Aung San Suu Kyi, won a landslide victory. Official results of the 1990 had the NLD winning 392 of the 485 contested seats in the new parliament. SLORC's party, the National Unity Party, won 10 seats. Two other opposition parties—the ethnic-based Shan Nationalities League for Democracy and the Arakan League for Democracy—won 23 and 11 seats, respectively.

Following the election, Aung San Suu Kyi and other opposition leaders pressed SLORC to accept the popular will and transfer power to the new parliament. SLORC responded by arresting many of the opposition leaders—many of whom had won a seat in the elections—and imposing ever more restraints of civil liberties.

THE CONSTITUTIONAL REFERENDUM OF 2008

On February 9, 2008, the SPDC announced a national referendum on its draft constitution was to be held in May 2008.[5] On the same day, the SPDC also declared, "In accordance with the forthcoming State Constitution, the multi-party democracy [sic] general elections will be held in 2010."[6]

On February 26, 2008, the SPDC released a new law governing "the approval of the draft constitution."[7] The law barred the following people from voting: members of religious orders; people of unsound mind; persons in prison or convicted of a crime; people illegally abroad; and foreigners. The law also allowed the postponement or dissolution of a vote "if [a] free and fair referendum may not be held stably due to natural disaster or situation affecting the security, or any other disaster." The SPDC began providing copies of the 194-page draft constitution to the public on April 9, 2008, at a cost of 1,000 kyat ($1.50) and announced the date for the referendum—May 10, 2008.

On May 2, 2008, Cyclone Nargis, a category 3 cyclone,[8] caused widespread damage across much of southern and central Burma. Initial reports estimated the death toll at 351 people, but that number quickly rose to over 22,500, with 41,000 people reported as missing.[9] Official Burmese figures were later revised to 84,537 dead and 53,836 missing.[10]

Despite the widespread destruction caused by Cyclone Nargis, the SPDC decided to not invoke the natural disaster provisions of the referendum law. On May 6, 2008, the SPDC announced that the vote on the proposed constitution would proceed as planned in most of Burma, but that the vote would be delayed until May 24, 2008, for most of the townships around Rangoon and in seven of the townships in the Irrawaddy region.[11] The SPDC's decision to proceed with the referendum was met with strenuous objection by Burma's leading opposition groups, as well as by the United States and several other nations.

There are conflicting accounts about the conduct and outcome of the referendum. The SPDC reported a heavy turnout on both dates, with few voting irregularities. Opposition groups say the turnout was comparatively light, with many reported cases of voting irregularities, such a pre-marked ballots, voter intimidation, and other techniques to influence the outcome of the referendum.[12] On May 29, 2008, the SPDC issued Announcement No. 7/2008, reporting that 98.12% of the 27,288,827 eligible voters had cast votes, and that 92.48% had voted in favor of the adoption of the constitution.[13] On the basis of these official results, the SPDC declared that the new constitution had been ratified.

KEY FEATURES OF THE 2008 CONSTITUTION[14]

The 2008 constitution is a 213-page, detailed document. It establishes the Republic of the Union of Myanmar as a perpetual union of seven states and seven regions[15] under "a genuine, disciplined multi-party democratic system." Although "the Sovereign power of the Union is derived from the citizens," the constitution also stipulates that one of its objectives is "enabling the Defence Services to be able to participate in the national political leadership role of the State."

The 2008 constitution creates three equal branches of the State—the legislative, executive, and judicial branches—under a parliamentary system. The legislative branch is empowered to consider and approve legislation. It is headed by a national parliament (*Pyidaungsu Hluttaw*) with two chambers—the Union Assembly (*Pyithu Hluttaw*), with a maximum of 440 members selected by districts based on population, and the National Assembly (*Amyotha Hluttaw*), with a maximum of 224 members selected by the regions or states. Members of the *Pyidaungsu Hluttaw* serve terms of five years. Each chamber is to select a Speaker from amongst its members. The constitution also creates Regional and State Hluttaws. In each of the Hluttaws, a quarter of the seats are to be appointed by the Commander-in-Chief of Burma's Defence Services.

Burma's President is the head of the executive branch. The President's two main powers are to enforce the law and to promulgate ordinances, subject to the approval of the national parliament. The President can also designate Ministries, enter into treaties, and take military action (including declaring war or making peace), subject to the assent of the national parliament.

The constitution also provides for two Vice Presidents. The President and two Vice Presidents are selected by the parliament as a whole after each chamber of the parliament separately nominates one candidate, and the members of the national parliament appointed by the Commander-in-Chief of Burma's Defence Services nominate a third candidate. The terms of office for the President and Vice Presidents are five years; they are limited to two terms in office.

Within the Executive Branch, the constitution also establishes the "National Defence and Security Council" (NDSC), consisting of the President; the two Vice Presidents; the Speakers of each chamber of the national parliament; the Commander-in-Chief and Deputy Commander-in-Chief of the Defence Services; and the Ministers of Border Affairs, Defence, Foreign Affairs, and Home Affairs. According to the constitution, the four Ministers on the NDSC must be active military personnel. Chapter XI of the constitution gives the President the authority, after coordinating with the NDSC, to declare a state of emergency in all or part of Burma, and transfer all legislative, executive, and judicial authority to the Commander-in-Chief of Defence Services.

Burma's judicial branch is to consist of a Supreme Court, High Courts for each of the 14 states or regions, and lower level courts. Justices of the Supreme Court are nominated by the President and approved by the parliament as a whole. Burma's constitution provides for a separate Constitutional Tribunal of the Union to adjudicate cases interpreting the constitution or determining the constitutionality of laws passed by the parliament.

The 2008 constitution sets a number of conditions on persons holding public office in all three branches of the government. These include age requirements, natural citizenship for any person and both of her/his parents, and minimum residency requirements. It also bars a person who has dual citizenship, or has a close relative who is a foreign national from holding public office, effectively preventing opposition leader Aung San Suu Kyi from running for office because she was married to a British citizen and has two sons who are British nationals. The constitution has additional disqualification conditions for serving in parliament, including: serving a prison term; having committed certain types of offenses; being of unsound mind; insolvency; membership in a religious order; and being a civil servant (with an exception for Defense Services personnel).

Under the 2008 constitution, national legislation is to be considered by both chambers of the parliament separately. If and when a common version of a bills is approved by both chambers, it is sent to the President for approval. The President can either approve the bill or return it to the parliament with comments for reconsideration. If the parliament approves the bill a second time, with or without incorporating the President's comments, it becomes law.

Chapter VIII lists the rights and duties of the citizens of Burma. It provides for and protects a wide variety of human and civil rights, with an occasional qualification. For example, the freedom of religion can be limited in cases where laws are passed "for the purpose of public welfare or reform." Another provision of the constitution forbids "the abuse of religion for political purposes." The constitution also allows the suspension of certain civil liberties at times of war, foreign invasion, or insurrection.

Chapter IX of the constitution contains provisions governing elections. Suffrage is provided to all Burmese citizens 18 years old or older, regardless of ethnicity with a few notable exceptions. People who are members of religious orders, serving prison sentences, declared of unsound mind, insolvent or otherwise declared ineligible based on election laws are disenfranchised. Chapter IX also establishes the Union Election Commission, which is responsible for the conducting, supervising and determining the results of parliamentary (*hluttaw*) elections.

The constitution includes a separate chapter (Chapter X) regarding political parties. In particular, the constitution requires political parties to register with the government, and abide by the constitution and laws of the country. It also prohibits political parties from receiving direct and indirect "assistance from a foreign government, a religious association, other association or a person from a foreign country."

To amend the major provisions of the constitution requires the approval of over 75% of the members of the parliament as a whole, which effectively gives the military veto power over constitutional amendments.

THE 2010 ELECTIONS

The date on which the 2010 parliamentary elections are to be held has not yet been announced by the SPDC. The military junta released five laws on March 9, 2010, that will govern the conduct of the 2010 election. They are: (1) a law establishing the Union Election Commission; (2) a law setting the conditions for registering political parties to participate in the election; (3) a law concerning the election of the members of the *Pyithu Hluttaw*; (4) a law concerning the election of the members of the *Amyotha Hluttaw*; and (5) a law concerning the election of members of the state or regional *Hluttaws*. The new election laws have been sharply criticized by Burma's leading opposition groups. They also generally received a cool reception by the international community.

The Election Laws and Regulations[16]

Most of the controversy surrounding Burma's new election laws has focused on certain provisions in the law on political parties and the Union Election Commission. The three laws concerning the election of members of the various *hluttaws*, however, do contain provisions that have implications for the possibility of holding free and fair elections in Burma.

The Political Parties Registration Law

The Political Parties Registration Law requires that all political parties with 15 or more members register with the Union Election Commission. The party's registration must include the party's official name, flag, seal, constitution and regulations, party program and ideology, and detailed identification information about the party leadership. In its registration application, the political party must promise to safeguard and maintain the integrity of Burma, its constitution and its laws, as well as the "peace and tranquility" of the nation.

If a political party fails to register with the Union Election Commission within 60 days of the promulgation of the law—or, by May 7, 2010—the political party will be considered illegal and ineligible to participate in the 2010 election. Political parties must also contest in at least three constituencies in the general election for the *hluttaws*.

The law prohibits political parties from "directly or indirectly using money, buildings, vehicles and property owned by the State," as well as "directly or indirectly the support of money, land, housing, buildings, vehicles, property, so forth" from governments, religious organizations or other organizations of foreign countries. In addition, political parties cannot "abuse religion for political purposes."

The law also sets conditions on who can be a member of a political party. A person must be a Burmese citizen at least 18 years old to join a political party.[17] A person can only join one political party. Among the more controversial conditions set on party membership are: members of religious orders are prohibited; civil servants are prohibited; persons serving prison terms are prohibited; and persons with foreign citizenship are prohibited. Political parties that intentionally conceal prohibited party members may be deregistered by the Union Election Commission. The Union Election Commission also has the power to audit the financial records of political parties.

Union Election Commission Law

As required by the constitution, the law creates the Union Election Commission, and gives it the authority to supervise the *hluttaw* elections and Burma's political parties. The Union Election Commission has the power to create subcommissions, delineate constituencies, compile voting lists, certify election results, and form Election Courts to hear electoral disputes. The decisions of the Union Election Commission are final, and cannot be appealed to Burma's judicial courts.

A member of the Union Election Commission must be at least 50 years old; be determined to have a "good reputation among the people" by the SPDC; possess dignity and integrity; be "well-experienced," and be "loyal to the State and its citizens." Commission members cannot be a member of a political party, hold any office, or draw a "salary, allowances, or supplements."

The Hluttaw Election Laws

The other three laws released on March 9, 2010—the Amyotha Hluttaw Election Law, the Pyithu Hluttaw Election Law, and the Region Hluttaw or State Hluttaw Election Law—confirm the number of seats for each type of hluttaw, establish qualifications for eligible voters, set criteria for candidates, and specify other provisions related to the conduct of the elections.

The Amyotha Hluttaw Election Law stipulates that there will be 12 representatives from each Region or State, and 56 members appointed by the Commander-in-Chief of the Defense Services. The Pyithu Hluttaw Election Law provides for 330 seats which are to be elected based on Burma's townships, and 110 to be selected by the Commander-in-Chief of the Defense Services. The size of the Region or State Hluttaws is determined by a process that includes at least two representatives from each township, members elected based on Burma's recognized "national races," and members appointed by Commander-in-Chief of the Defense Services.

To vote in the parliamentary elections, a person must be a Burmese citizen at least 18 years old and listed on the constituency's electoral role. Foreigners or naturalized citizens of other countries; members of religious orders; and people serving prison terms, insolvent, or "adjudged to be of unsound mind" are not entitled to vote.

Each hluttaw law sets a minimum age for representatives. For the Amyotha Hluttaw, representatives must be 30 years old or older. For the Pyithu Hluttaw, and the Region or State Hluttaws, the minimum age is 25. All Hluttaw representatives must have been residing in Burma for a minimum of at least 10 continuous years prior to the election. Residency exemptions are provided for individuals residing overseas in an official capacity for the government. In addition, both of the candidate's parents must have been Burmese citizens at the time of their birth.

The Election Commission

Three days after releasing the five election laws, the SPDC announced the 17 members of the Union Election Commission.[18] According to the opposition newspaper, the *Irrawaddy*, "The majority of the chosen members are retired government officials who served under the ruling junta and took retirement in recent years."[19] Several of the members of the Union Election Council—including its Chairman U Thein Soe—are or have been on the European Union's sanction list of Burmese officials who are not allowed access into the European Union and/or whose assets are frozen. One of the election commission members—Aung Myint—appears on the U.S. Treasury's "Special Designated Nationals" list.[20]

The Response in Burma

The initial response in Burma to the five election laws and the list of appointees to the Union Election Commission was mostly negative. In the weeks since the laws' release, several leading political parties—including the National League for Democracy (NLD)—have decided not to participate in the election. However, there have been a number of political parties that have submitted the required registration materials, including some ethnic-based parties.

Burmese Comments on the Election Laws

Burmese criticism has largely focused on various provisions that effectively barred or inhibited the participation of leading opposition figures, such as Aung San Suu Kyi. Opposition leaders who are serving prison sentences (such as Aung San Suu Kyi) cannot run for office, vote in the elections or be members of political parties. People who have lived overseas any time during the last 10 years cannot run for office, effectively eliminating the participation of Burma's leaders-inexile. Burma's politically-active Buddhist monks and nuns—key organizers of the protests of 2007[21]—are not allowed to join a political party, vote in the elections, or run for office.

Comments also pointed to a perceived bias in the Political Parties Registration Law against opposition parties. Political parties that violate restrictions—such as the restriction on party members or the prohibition on foreign financial support—may be declared illegal and prohibited from participating in the elections. In addition, the cost of registering a political party—300,000 kyat or about $300—plus 500,000 kyat ($500) per candidate, may inhibit the participation of Burma's poor.

The election laws are also viewed as favoring the military. In addition to setting aside at least 25% of the seats in every *hluttaw* for appointees by the Commander-in-Chief of the Defence Services, military personnel are the only government employees allowed to form political parties, vote, or run for office, increasing the likelihood that the military will constitute more than 25% of the *hluttaws*.

There has also been criticism of the Union Election Commission Law and the people appointed to the commission. To some, the membership of the commission and the lack of appeal to the commission's decisions effectively turn the Union Election Commission into an instrument that the SPDC will likely use to influence the election results.

Political Party Registration

The Political Party Registration Law requires all existing political parties that wish to participate in the 2010 elections to submit registration materials to the Union Election Commission (UEC) within 60 days; new political parties have 90 days to register, according to by-laws approved by the UEC. Since the law was promulgated, several political parties or groups have announced that they do not intend to register, while a number have submitted their registration materials (see "Status of Political Parties in Burma," below).

The NLD's central executive committee unanimously voted against participating in the 2010 elections on March 29, 2010.[22] The decision came a week after NLD leader Aung San Suu Kyi stated that she "would not even think of registering under these unjust laws."[23] In the weeks prior to Suu Kyi's statement, there were reported disagreements among the NLD leadership about participation in the election. NLD Chairman Aung Shwe and NLD spokesperson Khin Maung Swe reportedly supported registering the party, but NLD leader Win Tin, who was released from Insein Prison on September 23, 2008, after 19 years in jail, openly opposed registering the party.[24] On April 29, 2010, Aung San Suu Kyi and the NLD filed an appeal to Burma's Supreme Court to annul the provisions in the Political Party Registration Law that would require the NLD to reregister as a political party to participate in the 2010 elections. The Supreme Court announced its decision not to hear the case on May 6, 2010.

The decision of the NLD not to register may have a far-reaching impact on the credibility of the 2010 elections. Political parties or groups have apparently been influenced by the NLD's decision and have subsequently stated they will not participate in the election. The Mon National Democratic Front, for example, voted not to register for the election the day after the NLD made its decision. Two weeks after the NLD's decision, only one of the top five parties to win seats in the 1990 elections had indicated it would participate in the 2010 election, the pro-junta National Unity Party, while three of the top five parties—the NLD, the Arakan League for Democracy and the Mon National Democratic Front—had decided not to participate. Given that these three parties won over 84% of the seats in the 1990 elections, their decision not to participate has created a possibly large void in representing the political views of a substantial segment of the Burmese electorate.

Table 1. Status of Political Parties in Burma (numbers following party names indicate number of seats—out of a possible 485—won in the 1990 parliamentary election)

Parties or groups that have announced they will not register:	Parties that have registered:
• Arakan League for Democracy—11	• 88 Generation Students Youths - Union of Myanmar
• Arakan Liberation Party	• All Mon Region Democratic Party
• Arakan National Congress	• Chin National Party
• Chin National League for Democracy—3	• Chin Progressive Party
• Kachin Independent Organization	• Democratic Party - Myanmar—1
• Kachin National Organization	• Democracy and Peace Party
• Democratic Karen Buddhist Army	• Difference and Peace Party
• Karen National Union/Karen National Liberation Army Peace Council	• Ethnic National Development Party
• Karenni National Progressive Party	• Inn National Development Party
• Kayan New Land Party	• Kachin State Progressive Party
• Mara People's Party—1	• Kayan National Party
• Mon National Democratic Front—5	• Kayin People's Party [a.k.a. Karen-People Party]
• National League for Democracy—392	• Kokang Democracy & Unity Party
• New Mon State Party	• Lahu National Development Party—1
• Shan Nationalities League for Democracy—23	• Mro or Khami National Solidarity Organization—1
• Zomi National Congress—2	• Myanmar New Society Democratic Party
	• National Democratic Party for Development
	• National Political Alliances League

Table 1. (Continued)

Parties or groups that have announced they will not register:	Parties that have registered:
	• National Unity Party—10
	• New Era People's Party
	• Northern Shan State Progressive Party
	• Pa-O National Organization—3
	• Phalon-Sawaw Democratic Party [a.k.a. Pwo-Sgaw]
	• Democratic Party]
	• Rakhine Nationals Progressive Party
	• Rakhine State National Force of Myanmar
	• Shan Nationals Democratic Party
	• Taaung (Palaung) National Party
	• Union Democracy Party
	• Union Kayin League [a.k.a. Union Karen League]
	• Union of Myanmar Federation of National Politics
	• Union Solidarity and Development Party
	• United Democratic Party
	• United Democracy Party (Kachin State)
	• Wa Democratic Party
	• Wa National Unity Party
	• Wunthanu National League for Democracy

Source: *New Light of Myanmar, The Irrawaddy, Mizzima*

There are also signs that the NLD decision has spawned a campaign to boycott the election. During the campaign for the constitutional referendum, there was a difference of opinion among the opposition groups on whether people should refuse to vote or vote against the constitution. With several of the leading opposition parties refusing to participate in the 2010 parliamentary election, there is a growing call for people not to vote to express their opposition to the new constitution and the election.

On April 29, 2010, the Union Solidarity and Development Party (USDP) submitted its application to the UEC, listing among its members 27 ex-military officers, including Prime Minister General Thein Sein.[25] It is unclear if the officers' resignations from the military is sufficient to comply with the provisions of the Political Party Registration Law, or if they also must resign from their ministerial positions. If successful in their application to form a political party, this move increases the chances of the military controlling more than 25% of the seats in the parliament. During the daily press briefing on May 4, 2010, Assistant Secretary of State Philip J. Crowley indicated that while the United States would generally support military officers to "take off their uniform and pursue politics and government as civilians," it will wait to see what actions Burma will take to determine "whether this represents just wolves changing to sheep's clothing...."[26]

The International Response

The international response to the five election laws has varied from sharp criticism to mild expressions of disappointment. An official statement by U.N. Secretary-General Ban Ki-moon indicated that a preliminary assessment of the laws "suggests that they do not measure up to the international community's expectations of what is needed for an inclusive political process."[27] The statement also reiterated the Secretary-General's call for "fair, transparent and credible elections in which all citizens of Myanmar, including Daw Aung San Suu Kyi, can freely participate."[28]

The day after the election laws were released, U.S. Assistant Secretary of State Philip J. Crowley referred to the Political Parties Registration Law as "a step in the wrong direction."[29] He also stated that the State Department was "deeply disappointed" that the law excluded political participation by Burma's over 2,000 political prisoners, including Aung San Suu Kyi, as well as the law's apparent prohibition of Aung San Suu Kyi continuing to be a member of the NLD, if it registers as a political party. Crowley concluded by saying, the law "makes a mockery of the democratic process and ensures that the upcoming elections will be devoid of creditability."[30]

Several other foreign leaders have expressed dissatisfaction or disappointment with the Burmese election laws. Britain's Prime Minister Gordon Brown said of the election laws, "Sadly, the Burmese regime has squandered the opportunity for national reconciliation."[31] Australia's Foreign Minister Stephen Smith told reporters, "I don't believe that any election without the National League for Democracy can be a full, free and fair election."[32] The Philippine's Foreign Secretary Alberto Romulo stated that the actions of the SPDC were "contrary to the roadmap to democracy that they have pledged to ASEAN and to the world."[33] Japan's Foreign Minister Katsuya Okada has indicated that Japan may cancel its plan to expand economic aid to Burma unless Aung San Suu Kyi and other opposition figures are permitted to participate in the 2010 elections.[34]

Some nations have been more restrained in their comments about Burma's election laws. Indonesia's Foreign Minister Marty Natalegawa traveled to Burma in late March to discuss the 2010 elections with Burma's Foreign Minster Nyan Win. Following their meetings, Natalegawa stated "We are trying very hard to ascertain as to what extent this sets [sic] of laws are consistent or inadvertently impede the holding of a multi-party election, an inclusive one and the likes."[35] Singapore's Foreign Ministry issued a similar statement, expressing its hope that "it is not too late for all parties to reach a compromise."[36]

On March 24, 2010, the U.N. Security Council held a closed-door meeting on the Burmese elections. It has been reported that Britain and China clashed over the appropriateness of the body to weigh in on the issue.[37] The following day, the informal Group of Friends of Burma[38] met and agreed that Burma's military junta should release all political prisoners (including Aung San Suu Kyi) and allow them to participate in the 2010 elections.[39] The Association of Southeast Asian Nations (ASEAN) released a statement following its April 9, 2010, leaders meeting, stating, "We underscored the importance of national reconciliation in Myanmar and the holding of the general election in a free, fair, and inclusive manner, thus contributing to Myanmar's stability and development."[40]

The SPDC's Response

Burma's ruling military junta has used its state-run newspaper, *The New Light of Myanmar*, to rebut some of the criticisms leveled at its election laws, generally by pointing to similarities in other nation's election laws. On March 27 and 28, 2010, the newspaper ran a two-part article written by "A Lawman" enumerating a response to "widespread criticism."[41] Regarding the powers of the Union Election Commission to oversee the political parties, the article points out that Indonesia grants its election commission similar powers. On the disenfranchisement of people serving prison terms, the article notes that in some countries, people are not allowed to vote for five or six years after their release from prison. It also recalls that Burma's 1947 constitution also had a provision prohibiting people from serving in the parliament for five years after their release from prison. As to members of religious orders, the SPDC has pointed out that past Burmese constitutions and election laws contained similar prohibitions on their participation in elections.

In his address at Burma's 65th Anniversary Armed Forces Day Parade, Senior General Than Shwe, SPDC Chairman and Commander-in-Chief of Defence Services, told the audience that "preparations are being made to be ready in every aspect for a gentle transition to democracy and market-oriented economic system."[42] He went on to warn that "the improper practice of democracy often leads to anarchic phenomena." Because Burma's democratic transition was only in its initial stages, Than Shwe asked that Burma's political parties "show restraint at a time when the democratization process has yet to reach maturity."

THE OBAMA ADMINISTRATION'S BURMA POLICY

In September 2009, the Obama Administration announced a change in U.S. policy towards Burma after seven months of review, discussion, and consultation. The new element to the Obama policy is the willingness to engage in direct dialogue with the SPDC on how to promote democracy and human rights in Burma, and greater cooperation on international security issues, such as nuclear nonproliferation and counternarcotics efforts.

Outside of the new willingness to engage in direct dialogue, the Obama policy is mostly a continuation of the policies of the two preceding administrations with the same goals—supporting "a unified, peaceful, prosperous, and democratic Burma that respects the human rights of its citizens."[43] In order to achieve these goals, the Obama Administration will continue to press Burma to release all its political prisoners, end all its conflicts with ethnic minorities, cease its human rights violations, and initiate "a credible internal political dialogue with the democratic opposition and ethnic minority leaders on elements of reconciliation and reform."[44] The existing U.S. sanctions on Burma—as stipulated in section 570 of the Omnibus Consolidated Appropriations Act, 1997; Burmese Freedom and Democracy Act of 2003; the Tom Lantos Block Burmese JADE Act of 2008; and a series of executive orders[45]—will remain in place "until we see concrete progress towards reform."[46] The Obama Administration also reserves the right to implement or recommend additional, targeted sanctions if warranted by circumstances inside Burma. The Obama policy will continue the past practice of cooperating with the international community to foster the desired changes inside Burma, including an intensified effort to engage with ASEAN, China, and India.

Since its announcement of a new Burma policy, the Obama Administration has held several direct discussions with SPDC officials, including the first ASEAN-U.S. leaders meeting in Singapore on November 15, 2009, which both President Obama and the SPDC's Chairman Than Shwe attended. A few days prior to the ASEAN-U.S. leaders meeting, U.S. Assistant Secretary of State for East Asia and the Pacific Kurt Campbell and Deputy Assistant Secretary of State Scot Marciel traveled to Burma to meet with Burma's Prime Minister Thein Sein—the highest level U.S. delegation to visit Burma in 14 years.[47] Campbell and Marciel also met with Aung San Suu Kyi and leaders of other opposition parties and ethnic minorities. Assistant Secretary of State Campbell also visited Burma on May 9-10, 2010, and had meetings with SPDC officials, NLD leaders (including Aung San Suu Kyi), and leaders from various ethnic minority groups.

Since the adoption of the new Burma policy, the SPDC has taken a series of steps contrary to the stated U.S. goals in Burma, including the promulgation of the five election laws. When asked during the State Department's daily press briefing on March 10, 2010, for signs of progress in Burma that have come out of the new policy, Assistant Secretary Philip J. Crowley stated that "so far, those results are lacking."[48]

After Crowley's comment, the SPDC decided to release and return U.S. citizen Kyaw Zaw Lwin (aka Nyi Nyi Aung). On February 10, 2010, a Burmese court convicted Kyaw on what the U.S. government considered "politically motivated charges,"[49] and sentenced him to three years in jail. Kyaw was released from Insein Prison on March 18, 2010, and returned to the United States.

Despite the apparent lack of progress towards achieving U.S. goals in Burma, Crowley informed the press in March 2010, "We are going to continue to have discussions with Burma, and I'm sure that in a variety of different fora others will have the same kind of discussion. I doubt that we're the only ones who are disappointed with the direction that they're taking at this point."[50] Assistant Secretary Campbell reportedly said on April 14, 2010, "We do think we have been able to pass some consequential messages but overall, I would say that we are going to need to see some steps on the part of the leadership in (Burma) to sustain this process going forward."[51] Following his May 2010 trip to Burma, Assistant Secretary Campbell stated that the Obama Administration was "profoundly disappointed by the response of the Burmese leadership."[52]

Congressional Concerns

There are also signs of disappointment in the Burmese government's behavior among some members of Congress. Nine Senators sent a letter to President Obama on March 26, 2010, urging the imposition of additional economic sanctions on the SPDC in light of the "a set of profoundly troubling election laws...."[53] The letter specifically asks the President to fulfill four provisions of the Tom Lantos Block Burmese JADE Act of 2008 (P.L. 110-286): (1) the appointment of a special representative and policy coordinator for Burma; (2) the imposition of additional banking sanctions; (3) the submission by the Secretary of the Treasury to certain congressional committees of a report "containing a list of all countries and foreign banking institutions that hold assets on behalf of senior Burmese officials"; and (4) the submission by the Secretary of State to certain congressional committees of a report on countries, companies, and other entities that provide military or intelligence aid to the SPDC. Both of the reports mentioned in the letter were due no later than 180 days after the enactment of the law, and annually thereafter.

Also, following the release of Burma's election laws, Senator Mitch McConnell issued a press release stating:

> The edict issued by Burma's State Peace and Development Council (SPDC) guarantees a profoundly undemocratic election by a profoundly undemocratic regime. If initial reports are accurate, it is no surprise that the law is a complete farce. By prohibiting Aung San Suu Kyi, political prisoners and Buddhist monks from participation, the junta makes clear that the only purpose of the upcoming election is simply to keep the SPDC in power.[54]

Congressional disappointment with recent SPDC actions is not limited to the election laws. For example, following the release of Kyaw Zaw Lwin, Senator John Kerry released the following statement:

> Sadly, while he is coming home, Burma's junta continues to hold its grip on 2,200 political prisoners.... In concert with our friends and partners in East Asia and around the world, the United States must redouble its efforts to persuade the junta to open discussions with the opposition and ethnic groups, to conduct genuinely free and fair elections, and to honor the aspirations of the Burmese people for a peaceful transition to democratic rule.[55]

Some in Congress discern other points of progress in Burma over recent months. For example, Senator Jim Webb had a different interpretation of

Kyaw Zaw Lwin's release and recent events in Burma, stating "Since my visit to Burma last August, the military government has made several substantive gestures that should be appropriately considered by the U.S. Department of State as opportunities to increase our engagement with Burma."[56]

Steps Taken

The 111th Congress has already taken steps to help achieve U.S. goals in Burma. Title III of Consolidated Appropriations Act, 2010 (P.L. 111-117) bans debt restructuring assistance to Burma until the Secretary of the Treasury "determines and notifies the Committees on Appropriations that a democratically elected government has taken office." Section 7071 of the law also requires the Secretary of Treasury to instruct the U.S. representative to all international financial institutions to which the United States is a member to "oppose and vote against the extension by such institution of any loan or financial or technical assistance or any other utilization of funds of the respective bank to and for Burma." In addition, the law provides "no less than $36,500,000" to support democracy and humanitarian programs in Burma, and that any new programs supported by these funds "shall only support activities that are consistent with the principles and goals of the National League for Democracy in Burma."[57]

In July 2009, the 111th Congress passed H.J.Res. 56 (P.L. 111-42) renewing the Burmese Freedom and Democracy Act of 2003 (P.L. 108-6 1) through 2012 and extending the trade sanctions for another year. Also, the Supplemental Appropriations Act, 2009 (P.L. 111-32) provided $10,000,000 for humanitarian assistance for individuals and communities impacted by Cyclone Nargis. In addition, on May 21, 2009, the Senate passed S.Res. 160 condemning and deploring the "show trial" of Aung San Suu Kyi, calling for the release of all political prisoners, and pressing the SPDC to "establish, with the full and unfettered participation of the National League for Democracy and ethnic minorities, a genuine roadmap for the peaceful transition to civilian, democratic rule." On May 7, 2010, the Senate passed by unanimous consent S.Res. 480 that, among other things, called upon "the Secretary of State to assess the effectiveness of the policy of engagement with the military regime in Burma in furthering United States interests...."[58]

Pending Resolutions

Three other resolutions have been introduced in the 111th Congress pertaining to Burma, and are awaiting possible action. H.Res. 898, introduced on November 6, 2009, extends the list of actions to be taken to promote democracy in Burma, adding such items as full implementation of the JADE Act of 2008, a U.N. resolution imposing multilateral sanctions and complete arms embargo of Burma, and a call for the Administration to support a U.N. Security Council Commission of Inquiry to investigate the Burmese regime's war crimes, crimes against humanity, and system of impunity. S.Res. 311, introduced on November 13, 2009, calls for the Administration to initiate negotiations for a free trade agreement with ASEAN, but stipulates:

> any pending bilateral issues between the United States and Burma, including economic sanctions, investment prohibition, travel restrictions or otherwise, should not deter the United States from engaging with other ASEAN nations regarding a potential free trade agreement, nor should the United States encourage trade with Burma, absent significant reforms within that country.

S.J.Res. 29 was introduced on May 5, 2010. It would renew the import restrictions contained in the Burmese Freedom and Democracy Act of 2003. According to Senator McConnell, one of the resolution's co-sponsors, renewing the sanctions was timely and important because, over the past year, the SPDC had given no clear indication that it intends to reform, but instead is "to stand up a new sham constitution and to legitimize itself in the eyes of the world through a sham election."[59]

Possible Additional Congressional Actions on Burma

If the 111th Congress were to take additional actions regarding Burma, there are several options available. However, prior to taking any action, Members would have to decide whether applying more or less pressure on the SPDC is more likely to advance the achievement of U.S. goals in Burma.

As indicated, there are differences of opinion in the 111th Congress on the current situation in Burma, and whether circumstances warrant the application of more or less pressure on the ruling military junta. There are also differing opinions in the international community on whether recent events indicate progress or regress in Burma's transition to democratic civilian rule. The views of other nations may be an important factor in the effectiveness of possible additional actions taken by Congress.

One possible action would be to hold hearings on the situation in Burma. The House Committee on Foreign Affairs held a hearing on Burma on October 21, 2009; the Senate Committee on Foreign Relations held a hearing on Burma on September 30, 2009. New hearings on topics such as the upcoming Burmese elections may be useful in deciding if additional congressional action is warranted.

A second possible course of action would be to press the Obama Administration to fully enforce the provisions of the Burmese Freedom and Democracy Act of 2003 and the Tom Lantos Block Burmese JADE Act of 2008. In addition to the four provisions mentioned in the Senators' March 2010 letter to President Obama, there are other provisions in the two laws that have not been fully implemented. For example, section 6 of the Burmese Freedom and Democracy Act of 2003 requires the Secretary of State to post on the Department of State's website the names of past and present SPDC and USDA leaders whose entry into the United States is banned under the law. Similarly, section 5(d) of the Tom Lantos Block Burmese JADE Act of 2008 requires the President to submit to the "appropriate congressional committees" a list of sanctioned Burmese officials as defined by the provisions of the act. As of the writing of this chapter, neither list has been supplied as required.

A third possible course of action would be to enact new sanctions on Burma, if the 111th Congress determines that *increasing* pressure on the SPDC is warranted. There are a wide range of options for additional sanctions, some which have been mentioned or alluded to in existing legislation. Some examples are: a ban on the import of products containing timber or lumber from Burma; prohibiting "United States persons" from entering into economic-financial transactions, paying taxes, or performing "any contract" with Burmese government institutions or individuals under U.S. sanctions; requiring all U.S. entities to divest their investments and cease operations in Burma; and restricting the provision of transactional services to foreign financial institutions that hold assets on behalf of senior Burmese officials.

A fourth possible course of action, if the 111th Congress determines that *decreasing* pressure on the SPDC is warranted, would be to remove or reduce some of the existing sanctions on Burma.[60] It should be noted that the laws governing many of the existing sanctions contain provisions allowing for a presidential waiver if the President determines that doing so is in national interest of the United States.

APPENDIX. MAP OF BURMA (MYANMAR)

The United States officially refers to the country as Burma, and recognizes Rangoon as its capital. The SPDC officially renamed their country, "the Union of Myanmar," in 1989 and relocated the capital to Nay Pyi Taw in 2005.

Source: CRS.

ACKNOWLEDGMENTS

This chapter was prepared with the assistance of Nese DeBruyne, Information Research Specialist, 7-8096.

End Notes

[1] The 1990 parliamentary election was an overwhelming victory for the National League for Democracy (NLD) and its leader, Aung San Suu Kyi. However, following the announcement of the results of the election, Burma's ruling military junta refused to transfer power to civilian power. For more information, see James F. Guyot, "Myanmar in 1990: The Unconsummated Election," *Asian Survey*, Vol. 31, No. 2, (Feb. 1991), pp. 205-211.

[2] For more information regarding Cyclone Nargis and Burma's constitutional referendum, see CRS Report RL34481, *Cyclone Nargis and Burma's Constitutional Referendum*, by Michael F. Martin and Rhoda Margesson.

[3] It was not the only hiatus for the National Convention. For example, it adjourned in January 1993 after delegates refused to endorse a clause stating that the military had a leading role in Burma's political system. The National Assembly remained in recess until November 1995.

[4] The phrase, "disciplined democracy," or close variations of it, have been used by SDPC leaders in speeches since Khin Nyunt's speech laying out the seven-step roadmap to democracy on August 30, 2003.

[5] State Peace and Development Council, Announcement No. 1/2008, February 9, 2008, available at http://www.mewashingtondc.com/Myanmar %202%20of%202008.pdf.

[6] State Peace and Development Council, Announcement No. 2/2008, February 9, 2008, available at http://www.mewashingtondc.com/Myanmar %202%20of%202008.pdf.

[7] "The Referendum Law for the Approval of the Draft Constitution of the Republic of the Union of Myanmar," official translation published in *The New Light of Myanmar*, February 28, 2008, pages 8-11.

[8] Tropical storms in the Indian Ocean are generally referred to as cyclones, whereas tropical storms in the western Pacific Ocean are referred to as typhoons and in the eastern Pacific Ocean and the Atlantic Ocean, they are called hurricanes. A category 3 cyclone has "very destructive" winds with gusts of 170-225 kph (105-14 1 mph).

[9] "Hundreds Killed by Burma Cyclone," *BBC*, May 4, 2008; Aye Aye Win, "Nearly 4,000 People Dead; 3,000 People Missing," *Associated Press*, May 5, 2008; "Burmese Storm Toll 'Tops 10,000,'" *BBC*, May 5, 2008; "Burma's Cyclone Death Toll Soars," *BBC*, May 6, 2008, and Aung Hla Tun, "Myanmar Cyclone Toll Climbs to Nearly 22,500," *Reuters*, May 6, 2008.

[10] "84,500 Confirmed Death from Cyclone Nargis," *Associated Press*, June 24, 2008; and "Official: Myanmar Cyclone Death Toll Mounts to 84,537," *Xinhua*, June 24, 2008.

[11] Jocelyn Gecker, "Vote Delayed in a Few Worst Cyclone-hit Areas but the Rest Will Go Ahead," *Associated Press*, May 6, 2008.

[12] The human rights organization, *Dictator Watch*, reported on March 26, 2010, that a Burmese military officer claims to have actively participated in vote rigging in the 2008 referendum by destroying "no" votes and replacing them with false "yes" votes. According to the officer, over 50% of the authentic ballots were marked "no." The officer also claims that the SPDC plans on using similar techniques to rig the 2010 parliamentary elections. For more details, see Roland Watson, "Intelligence from Burma Police Defector," *Dictator Watch*, March 26, 2010.

[13] "Myanmar Ratifies and Promulgates Constitution," *New Light of Myanmar*, May 30, 2008.

[14] Citations in this section are from an official English version of the 2008 constitution published by Burma's Ministry of Information, available on*line at* http://burmadigest.info/wp-content/uploads/2008/11/myanmar_constitution-2008- en.pdf.

[15] The seven states are Chin, Kachin, Kayah, Kayin, Mon, Rakhine, and Shan; the seven regions are Ayeyawady, Bago, Magway, Mandalay, Sagaing, Taninthayi, and Yangon. The constitution also provides that the new capital Nay Pyi Taw be designated as a "Union territory" under the direct administration of Burma's President.

[16] Citations of Burmese elections laws in this section are unofficial translations provided by Network Myanmar (www.networkmyanmar.org).
[17] Citizens include native-born, naturalized or guest citizens, or holders of temporary identification documents.
[18] An English translation of the announcement was published in the March 12, 2010, edition of *the New Light of Myanmar,* the SPDC-run newspaper.
[19] "Election Commission Members from Various Backgrounds," *The Irrawaddy,* March 12, 2010.
[20] A separate "visa ban" list that is supposed to be maintained by the State Department under the provisions of the Burmese Freedom and Democracy Act of 2003 has not been made available to the public and Congress. Also, the apparent discrepancy between the E.U. and U.S. list brings into question compliance with section 5(d)(2) of the Tom Lantos Block Burmese JADE Act of 2008, that requires the President to consider "data already obtained by other countries and entities that apply sanctions against Burma, such as the Australian Government and the European Union."
[21] In the autumn of 2007, a series of popular protests swept across Burma. Initially a response to economic measures implemented by the SPDC, the nature of the protests shifted after Burmese soldiers shot and killed a number of Buddhist monks participating in a peaceful march. The protests were quelled by the end of September, after an unknown number of deaths and the detention of several thousand protesters, including hundreds of Buddhist monks. For more information about the 2007 protests, see CRS Congressional Distribution Memo CD07 1227, "Background Information on the Recent Protests in Burma and Their Aftermath," December 20, 2007, by Michael F. Martin.
[22] Aung Hla Tun, "Suu Kyi's Party Says Won't Stand in Myanmar Polls," *Reuters,* March 30, 2010.
[23] Ba Kuang, "Suu Kyi Against NLD Joining Elections," *The Irrawaddy,* March 23, 2010.
[24] Ba Kaung, "Divisions over Party Registration Surfacing in NLD," *The Irrawaddy,* March 17, 2010.
[25] Kyaw Kha, "PM, Now a Retired General, Leads USDA Party," *Mizzima,* April 30, 2010.
[26] U.S. Department of State, "Daily Press Briefing," press release, May 4, 2010.
[27] United Nations Office of the Spokesperson for the Secretary-General, "Statement attributable to the Spokesperson for the Secretary-General on Myanmar," press release, March 10, 2010.
[28] Ibid. Note—the term "Daw" is an honorific, and not part of her name.
[29] U.S. Department of State, "Daily Press Briefing," press release, March 10, 2010.
[30] Ibid.
[31] Aung Zaw, "Hipocrisy Replaces Hope after the NLD Decision," *The Irrawaddy,* March 31, 2010.
[32] Ibid.
[33] "Philippines: Burma Broke Promise to Democratize," *Associated Press,* March 16, 2010.
[34] "Okada: Let Suu Kyi Run in Elections or No Aid," *Japan Times,* March 28, 2010.
[35] "Indonesia Shares Its Experience with Myanmar on Road to Democracy," *Channel News Asia,* April 8, 2010.
[36] Aung Zaw, "Hypocrisy Replaces Hope after NLD Decision," *The Irrawaddy,* March 31, 2010.
[37] "Security Council Mulls Myanmar's Election Laws," *AFP,* March 24, 2010.
[38] The Group of Friends of Burma is an informal consultative body organized by the U.N. Secretary-General to develop a shared approach to relations with Burma. The members of the group are Australia, Britain, China, the European Union, France, India, Indonesia, Japan, Norway, Russia, Singapore, South Korea, Thailand, the United States, and Vietnam.
[39] Bill Varner, "China Urges Burma to Free Political Prisoners," *Sydney Morning Herald,* March 27, 2010.
[40] Association of Southeast Asian Nations, "Chairman's Statement of the 16th ASEAN Summit 'Towards the ASEAN Community: from Vision to Action'," press release, April 9, 2010.

[41] A Lawman, "Not to Leave an Evil Legacy Behind," *New Light of Myanmar*, March 27 and 28, 2010.
[42] "This Year's Elections Represent Only Beginning of Process of Fostering Democracy," *New Light of Myanmar*, March 28, 2010.
[43] U.S. Department of State, "U.S. Policy Toward Burma," press release, September 28, 2010.
[44] Ibid.
[45] These include Executive Orders 13047, 13310, 13448, and 13464
[46] Ibid.
[47] Tim Johnston, "Scant Details on Reaction to U.S. Envoys' Burma Visit," *Washington Post*, November 6, 2009.
[48] U.S. Department of State, "Daily Press Briefing," press release, March 10, 2010.
[49] U.S. Department of State, "Burma: Conviction of Kyaw Zaw Lwin," press release, February 10, 2010.
[50] U.S. Department of State, "Daily Press Briefing," press release, March 10, 2010.
[51] Tim Johnston, "US Envoy Meets Burma's Aung San Suu Kyi," *Financial Times*, May 9, 2010.
[52] U.S. Embassy in Rangoon, Burma, "Assistant Secretary Campbell's Remarks on Visit to Burma," press release, May 10, 2010.
[53] "Letter to the President," March 26, 2010.
[54] Office of Senator Mitch McConnell, "Statement of Senator McConnell on Burma's Election Laws," press release, March 10, 2010.
[55] Office of Senator John Kerry, "Chairman Kerry Statement on the Release of American Citizen Held in Burma," press release, March 18, 2010.
[56] Office of Senator Jim Webb, "Statement of Senator Webb on the Release of American Citizen Kyaw Zaw Lwin in Burma," press release, March 18, 2010.
[57] The Omnibus Appropriations Act, 2009 (P.L. 111-8) contained similar provisions.
[58] S.Res. 480.
[59] Senator Mitch McConnell, "S.J. Res. 29. A joint resolution approving the renewal of import restrictions contained in the Burmese Freedom and Democracy Act of 2003; to the Committee on Foreign Relations," Statements on Introduced Bills and Joint Resolutions, *Congressional Record*, May 5, 2010, pp. S3169-S3170.
[60] For a summary of the economic sanctions on Burma, see CRS Report RS22737, *Burma: Economic Sanctions*, by Larry A. Niksch and Martin A. Weiss.

In: Bangladesh and Burma: Background and Issues ISBN: 978-1-61761-219-0
Editor: Brandon E. Stromberg © 2011 Nova Science Publishers, Inc.

Chapter 4

BURMA AND TRANSNATIONAL CRIME

Liana Sun Wyler

SUMMARY

Transnational organized crime groups in Burma (Myanmar) operate a multi-billion dollar criminal industry that stretches across Southeast Asia. Trafficked drugs, humans, wildlife, gems, timber, and other contraband flow through Burma, supporting the illicit demands of the region and beyond. Widespread collusion between traffickers and Burma's ruling military junta, the State Peace and Development Council (SPDC), allows organized crime groups to function with impunity. Transnational crime in Burma bears upon U.S. interests as it threatens regional security in Southeast Asia and bolsters a regime that fosters a culture of corruption and disrespect for the rule of law and human rights.

Congress has been active in U.S. policy toward Burma for a variety of reasons, including combating Burma's transnational crime situation. At times, it has imposed sanctions on Burmese imports, suspended foreign assistance and loans, and ensured that U.S. funds remain out of the regime's reach. The 110th Congress passed P.L. 110-286, the Tom Lantos Block Burmese JADE Act of 2008 (signed by the President on July 29, 2008), which imposes further sanctions on SPDC officials and prohibits the indirect importation of Burmese gems, among other actions. On the same day, the President directed the U.S. Department of Treasury to impose financial sanctions against 10 Burmese companies, including companies involved in the gem-mining industry, pursuant to Executive Order 13464 of April 30, 2008.

The second session of the 111th Congress may choose to conduct oversight of U.S. policy toward Burma, including the country's role in criminal activity. Secretary of State Hillary Clinton announced in February 2009 the beginning of a review of U.S.-Burma relations. In September 2009, the conclusions of this policy review were released, noting in particular the beginning of direct dialogue with Burmese authorities on international crime-related issues, including compliance with U.N. arms sanctions and counternarcotics. Already in the first session of the 111th Congress, both the Senate and the House have held hearings in which crime issues related to Burma have been addressed.

This chapter analyzes the primary actors driving transnational crime in Burma, the forms of transnational crime occurring, and current U.S. policy in combating these crimes. For further analysis of U.S. policy to Burma, see CRS Report RL33479, *Burma-U.S. Relations*, by Larry A. Niksch.

SCOPE OF THE PROBLEM

Transnational organized crime groups flourish in Burma, trafficking contraband that includes drugs, humans, guns, wildlife, gems, and timber. Transnational crime is highly profitable, reportedly generating roughly several billion dollars each year. The country's extra-legal economy, both black market and illicit border trade, is reportedly so large that an accurate assessment of the size and structure of the country's economy is unavailable. Contraband trafficking also remains a low-risk enterprise, as corruption among officials in Burma's ruling military junta, the State Peace and Development Council (SPDC), appears to facilitate trafficking and effectively provide the criminal underground immunity from law enforcement and judicial action.[1] Synergistic links connect various forms of contraband trafficking; smugglers use the same routes for many forms of trafficking, following paths of least resistance, where corruption and lax law enforcement prevail.

The continued presence of transnational crime in Burma and the illicit trafficking routes across Burma's borders share many features of so-called "ungoverned spaces"—regions of the world where governments have difficulty establishing control or are complicit in the corruption of the rule of law.[2] Among the commonalities that Burma's border regions share with other ungoverned spaces is physical terrain that is difficult to control. Burma's long borders, through which much smuggled contraband passes, stretch across vast trackless hills and mountains that are poorly patrolled. In addition, continuing ethnic tensions with some ethnic armed rebel groups hamper government control in some regions of the country, which is another common feature of ungoverned spaces. Recent cease-fire agreements in other border regions have not markedly improved the situation; instead, these cease-fires have provided groups known for their activity in transnational crime with near autonomy, essentially placing these areas beyond the reach of Burmese law.

Congress has long been active in U.S. policy toward Burma for a variety of reasons, including on issues related to transnational crime. Because the State Department lists Burma as a major drug- producing state, the country is barred access from U.S. foreign assistance under several longstanding legislative provisions.[3] Congress also authorizes sanctions against countries that the State Department deems in non-compliance with the minimum standards for the elimination of trafficking in persons, which includes Burma.[4]

The 110th Congress sought to strengthen unilateral sanctions against Burma. In response to the Burmese government's forced suppression of anti-regime protests in August and September of 2007, as well as its internationally criticized humanitarian response to destruction resulting from tropical cyclone Nargis in May 2008, Congress passed P.L. 110-286, the Tom Lantos Block Burmese JADE Act of 2008 (signed by the President on July 29, 2008). This law imposes further sanctions on SPDC officials and prohibits the indirect import of Burmese gems, among other actions. H.Rept. 110-418, which accompanies H.R. 3890, also cites "Burma's rampant drug trade" and "its role as a source for international trafficking in persons and illicit goods" as additional reasons for these new sanctions.

The 111th Congress may choose to continue its interest in oversight of U.S. policy toward Burma, including the country's role in criminal activity. Secretary of State Hillary Clinton announced in February 2009 the beginning of a review of U.S.-Burma relations. In September 2009, the conclusions of this policy review were released, noting in particular the beginning of direct dialogue with Burmese authorities on international crime-related issues, including compliance with U.N. arms sanctions and counternarcotics. Already in the first session of the 111th Congress, both the Senate and the House have held hearings in which crime issues related to Burma have been addressed.

PRIMARY ACTORS AND MOTIVES

Organized Crime, Ethnic Gangs, and Insurgent Groups

The United Wa State Army (UWSA), Shan State Army-South (SSA-S), Shan State Army-North (SSA-N), Democratic Karen Buddhist Army (DBKA), ethnic Chinese criminal groups (including the Triads), and other armed groups have criminal networks that stretch from India to Malaysia and up into China. Many of the transnational criminal elements along Burma's border are linked to past or ongoing ethnic insurgencies. While not necessarily a threat to SPDC control, they continue to constitute a transnational security threat for Burma and the region. The State Department states that the UWSA is the largest of the organized criminal groups in the region and operates freely along the China and Thailand borders, controlling much of the Shan State with a militia estimated to have 16,000 to 20,000 members.[5] Other criminal groups, including the 14K Triad, reportedly operate in the north of the country and in major population centers.[6] According to the Economist Intelligence Unit (EIU), these criminal organizations remain nearly immune from SPDC interference, because of widespread collusion with junta military, police, and political officials.[7] Many analysts agree that much of this apparent collusion is part of concerted SPDC efforts to coopt ethnic groups and avoid hostilities with them. One possible consequence of this policy is that the influence of organized crime in Burma and the region could remain virtually impossible to reduce.

Official Corruption

The U.S. State Department and other observers indicate that corruption is common among the bureaucracy and military in Burma. Burmese officials, especially army and police personnel in the border areas, are widely believed to be involved in the smuggling of goods and drugs, money laundering, and corruption.[8] Burma has no laws on record specifically related to corruption and has signed but not ratified the U.N. Convention against Corruption. The 2006 EIU country report on Burma states that "corruption and cronyism" are widespread "throughout all levels of the government, the military, the bureaucracy and business communities." Burma is reported to be the third-most corrupt country in the world according to Transparency International's

2009 *Corruption Perceptions Index*, after Somalia and Afghanistan.[9] In addition, the State Department states that Burma's weak implementation of anti-money laundering controls remains at the root of the continued use by narcotics traffickers and other criminal elements of Burmese financial institutions.[10] Burma has signed, but not ratified, the United Nations Convention against Corruption, which entered into force in December 2005.

Although there is little direct evidence of top-level regime members' involvement in trafficking- related corruption, there is evidence that high-level officials and Burmese military officers have benefitted financially from the earnings of transnational crime organizations. In the case of the drug trade, reports indicate Burmese military officials at various levels have several means to gain substantial shares of narcotics trafficking earnings. Some reports indicate that the Burmese armed forces, or *Tatmadaw*, may be directly involved in opium poppy cultivation in Burma's Shan state. Some local Tatmadaw units and their families reportedly work the poppy fields and collect high taxes from the traffickers, as well as fees for military protection and transportation assistance.[11] According to the State Department, Burma has not indicted any military official above the rank of colonel for drug-related corruption.[12]

The SPDC also reportedly allows and encourages traffickers to invest in an array of domestic businesses, including infrastructure and transportation enterprises, receiving start-up fees and taxes from these enterprises in the process. The traffickers usually deposit the earnings from these enterprises into banks controlled by the military, and military officers reportedly deposit much of their crime-related money in foreign bank accounts in places like Bangkok and Singapore.[13] In 2003, the Secretary of the Treasury reported that some Burmese financial institutions were controlled by, or used to facilitate money laundering for, organized drug trafficking organizations.[14] In the same report, the Secretary of the Treasury also stated that Burmese government officials were suspected of being involved in the counterfeiting of U.S. currency.

Possible links between drug trafficking operations and official corruption have been raised recently in the context of SPDC reconstruction contracts in the aftermath of cyclone Nargis. Specifically, some reports have pointed to SPDC's reconstruction contract with Asia World Company Ltd., a firm managed by Steven Law (Tun Myint Naing), as a possible indication of continued links between drug traffickers and official corruption.[15] Steven Law, against whom the U.S. government has maintained financial sanctions since February 2008, allegedly provides material support to the Burmese junta, receives business concessions from the junta, facilitates the movement of illicit narcotics, and launders drug profits through his firms, including Asia World Company Ltd. [16]

Regional Demand

The most frequent destinations for much of Burmese contraband—opium, methamphetamine, illegal timber, endangered wildlife, and trafficked humans—are China and Thailand.[17] Other destinations include India, Laos, Bangladesh, Vietnam, Indonesia, Malaysia, Brunei Darussalam, South Korea, and Cambodia. Demand for Burma's contraband reaches beyond the region, including the United States. The U.S. Drug Enforcement Administration (DEA), for example, reports that Burmese-trafficked methamphetamine pills have been confiscated within the United States.[18] The United States is also reputed to be among the world's largest importers of illegal wildlife;[19] no concrete data exist, however, to link such transnational ties with Burma.

Peasants and Urban Poor

Ready recruits for organized crime activities can be found in both urban ghettos and impoverished rural areas.[20] According to the Asian Development Bank, 27% of Burma's population live below the poverty line, making the country one of the poorest in Southeast Asia. Many analysts state that peasant farmers, rural hunters, and other poor often serve at the base of Burma's international crime network, growing opium poppy crops, poaching exotic and endangered species in Burma's lush forests, and serving as couriers and mules for contraband. In addition, the State Department and other observers have found that many victims of transnational crime in Burma are the poor, becoming commodities themselves as they are trafficked to be child soldiers for the junta or slaves for sexual exploitation.[21]

ILLICIT ECONOMIES IN BURMA

Drugs

Burma is party to all three major United Nations international drug control treaties—the 1961 Single Convention on Narcotic Drugs, as amended; the 1971 Convention on Psychotropic Substances; and the 1988 Convention against the Illicit Traffic in Narcotic Drugs and Psychotropic Substances. Burma's official strategy to combat drugs aims to end all production and trafficking of illegal drugs by 2014, a goal that parallels the region's ambition to be drug free by 2015.[22] Many analysts, however, consider the goal of achieving a drug-free Burma as unlikely. In September 2007, the Administration once again included Burma on the list of major drug transit or major illicit drug producing countries.[23] Located at the heart of the "Golden Triangle" of narcotics trafficking, Burma is among the world's top producers of opium, heroin, and methamphetamine.[24] Illicit narcotics reportedly generate between $1 billion and $2 billion annually in exports. In addition, Burma's drug trafficking activities appear to be linked to the recent spread of HIV and AIDS in the region, as drug users along Burma's trafficking routes share contaminated drug injection needles.

Some analysts warn that clashes between the government of Burma, rebel groups in the border areas of Burma, and neighboring countries could be possible. For example, should the SPDC begin to combat the drug trade more vigorously, current cease-fire groups may choose to break their agreements with the SPDC in order to protect their drug trade territories. Several cease-fire groups, including the UWSA, have chosen not to heed calls by the SPDC to disarm and reportedly use illicit drug proceeds to equip and maintain their paramilitary forces.[25] Beginning in June 2009 through at least late August 2009, the Burmese Army initiated a military campaign against several ethnic minority groups, including the Karen and the Kokang.[26] Thai counterdrug officials report a concurrent spike in heroin and methamphetamine sales in the region. It appears that various ethnic rebels are selling off their stockpiles of drugs in order to expand their weapons arsenals and prepare for the possibility of active conflict.[27]

Further, some suggest that the continued flow of illicit drugs from Burma to Thailand may be a source of tension between the two countries—especially in the face of Thailand's renewed war on drugs. The most recent campaign to combat illegal drugs, which began in April 2009, is a reprise of a 2003 campaign. Though media reports indicate that the current Thai war on drugs appears to be more restrained than the 2003 version, which resulted in the deaths of several thousand people over a three-month period, human rights activists remain on alert.[28]

Heroin and Opium

Burma is the world's second-largest producer of illicit opium, behind Afghanistan. Further, the DEA reports that Burma accounts for 80% of all heroin produced in Southeast Asia and is a source of heroin for the United States.[29] Although poppy cultivation has declined significantly in the past decade, prices have increased significantly in recent years, reflecting ongoing demand despite production declines since a decade ago (see **Table 1**). Some suggest that future dynamics of the opiate market in Burma may be dependent on developments in other opium-producing regions, particularly Afghanistan, which replaced Burma as the primary opium producer in the world.[30] Much of the decline in recent years has been attributed to UWSA's 2005 public commitment to stop its activity in the opium and heroin markets, after prolonged international pressure to do so. However, recent reports suggest that the UWSA's self-imposed ban may be short-lived. The UWSA has reportedly warned that alternative livelihood sources will be necessary in order to sustain its ban against opium poppy cultivation—a point with which many international observers agree.[31]

Most analysts acknowledge that opium production in certain parts of Burma is one of the few viable means for small-scale peasant farmers to compensate for structural food security shortages. A 2009 United Nations Office on Drugs and Crime (UNODC) study supports this, finding that households in former poppy-growing villages were unable to find sufficient substitutes for their lost income from opium.[32] According to the same UNODC study, the average annual cash income of a household involved in opium poppy cultivation was approximately $700, while the annual income of a household not involved in opium poppy cultivation was approximately $750. In Burma's Shan State in 2009, known for its pockets of opium production, 28% of poppy growing households (versus 22% of non-poppy growing households) reported food insecurity due to a shortage of rice.[33] In the meantime, reports indicate that opium poppy production is shifting to areas controlled by other cease-fire ethnic groups, and to areas apparently administered by Burma's armed forces, the Tatmadaw, who tax the farmers and traders for a portion of the farmgate value.[34] The UWSA may also be organizing Wa poppy farmers to seasonally migrate to nearby provinces, where the UWSA did not commit to a ban, in order to continue their cultivation.[35]

Methamphetamine and Synthetic Drugs

In addition to producing heroin and opium, Burma is reportedly the largest producer of methamphetamine in the world and a significant producer of other synthetic drugs.[36] Methamphetamine is produced in small, mobile labs in insurgent-controlled border areas, mainly in eastern Burma (for export mainly to Thailand) and sometimes co-located with heroin refineries.[37] Burma's rise to prominence in the global synthetic drug trade is in part the consequence of UWSA's commitment to ban opium poppy cultivation. According to some, UWSA leadership may be intentionally replacing opium cultivation with the manufacturing and trafficking of amphetamine-type stimulants.[38] As a result, Burma has emerged as one of the world's largest producers of methamphetamine and other amphetamine-type stimulants. The State Department states that this sharp increase in methamphetamine trafficking is "threatening to turn the Golden Triangle into an 'Ice Triangle.'"[39]

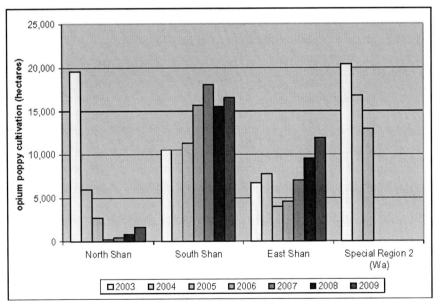

Source: UNODC, *Myanmar Opium Survey* (2007-2009).

Figure 1. Opium Poppy Cultivation in Burma's Shan State, 2003-2009

Table 1. Opium Cultivation, Production, and Price Trends in Burma, 1997-2009

Year	Opium Poppy Cultivation (hectares)	Significant Opium Poppy Eradication Reported (hectares)	Potential Opium Production (metric tons)	Total Potential Farm Gate Value of Opium Produced (U.S. constant dollars)
2009	31,700	4,087	330	$104 million
2008	28,500	4,820	410	$123 million
2007	27,700	3,598	460	$120 million
2006	21,500	3,970	315	$72 million
2005	32,800	3,907	312	$63 million
2004	44,200	2,820	370	$98 million
2003	62,200	7,469	810	$121 million
2002	81,400	9,317	828	$147 million
2001	105,000	1,643	1,097	$291 million
2000	108,700	9,824	1,087	$308 million
1999	89,500	3,172	895	$145 million
1998	130,300	3,093	1,303	$454 million
1997	155,150	1,938	1,676	$590 million

Source: CRS calculations based on United Nations Office on Drugs and Crime (UNODC), *World Drug Report*, 2004-2009; UNODC, *Opium Poppy Cultivation in South East Asia*, December 2008; and UNODC, *Global Illicit Drug Trends*, 2003-1999

A July 2008 media report indicates that international assistance for relief from the cyclone Nargis may have been used as a cover to smuggle illegal drugs into Burma. According to the *Irrawaddy*, an independent Burmese newspaper, several customs officials were suspected of involvement in a scheme to smuggle ecstasy pills into Burma as part of shipments of relief aid from Burmese communities abroad.[40]

Trafficking in Persons and Child Soldiers

Burma is a party to the United Nations Convention against Transnational Organized Crime and its protocol on migrant smuggling and trafficking in persons. However, Burma has been designated as a "Tier 3" state in every

Trafficking in Persons (TIP) Report ever published by the State Department. Tier 3 is the worst designation in the TIP Report, indicating that the country does not comply with minimum standards for combating human trafficking under the Trafficking Victims Protection Act of 2000, as amended (Division A of P.L. 106-386, 22 U.S.C. 7101, et seq.). As the TIP reports explain, laws to criminally prohibit sex and labor trafficking, as well as military recruitment of children, exist in Burma—and the penalties prescribed by these laws for those convicted of breaking these laws are "sufficiently stringent." Nevertheless, the State Department continues to report that these laws are arbitrarily enforced by the SPDC and that cases involving high-level officials or well-connected individuals are not fully investigated.

Victims are trafficked internally and regionally, and junta officials are directly involved in trafficking for forced labor and the unlawful conscription of child soldiers, according to several reports.[41] Women and girls, especially those of ethnic minority groups and those among the thousands of refugees along Burma's borders, are reportedly trafficked for sexual exploitation. Victims are reportedly trafficked from rural villages to urban centers and commerce nodes, such as truck stops, border towns, and mining and military camps.[42] One incident in early 2008 revealed the risks associated with migrant smuggling from Burma to Thailand, when 54 Burmese migrants were found dead in the back of a seafood truck headed to Thailand after the truck's air conditioning failed. Based on media accounts, 67 migrants survived, including at least 14 minors.[43]

In September 2009, the U.S. Department of Labor released a report and initial list of goods produced by child labor or forced labor. This is a congressionally mandated report, pursuant to the Trafficking Victims Protection Reauthorization Acts of 2005 and 2008, which required that the Department of Labor's Bureau of International Labor Affairs (DOL/ILAB) develop and publish a list of goods from countries in which ILAB had "reason to believe" were produced as a result of child or forced labor. Burma is listed among the 58 countries described in the ILAB report, with 14 separate production sectors implicated.[44]

Natural Resources

Timber and Wildlife

Burma is rich in natural resources, including extensive forests, high biodiversity, and deposits of minerals and gemstones. Illegal trafficking of these resources is reportedly flowing to the same destination states and along the same trafficking routes as other forms of trafficking. Global Witness, a London-based non-governmental organization, estimates that 98% of Burma's timber exports to China, from 2001 to 2004, were illegally logged, amounting to an average of $200 million worth of illegal exports each year.[45] Many analysts also claim that the region's illegal timber trade is characterized by complex patronage and corruption systems.[46]

Wild Asiatic black bears, clouded leopards, Asian elephants, and a plethora of reptiles, turtles, and other unusual animals reportedly are sold in various forms—whole or in parts, stuffed, ground, or, sometimes, alive—in open-air markets in lawless border towns.[47] Growing demand in countries such as China and Thailand has increased regional prices for exotic wildlife; for example, a tiger's skin can be worth up to $20,000, according to media reports.[48] One report suggests that valuable wildlife is used as currency in exchange for drugs and in the laundering of other contraband proceeds.[49]

Gems

Rubies, sapphires, jade, and other gems have also been used as non-cash currency equivalents for transborder smuggling. The legal sale of Burmese gems is among the country's most significant foreign currency earners—$297 million during the 2006-2007 fiscal year, according to Burma's customs department; more may be traded through illicit channels.[50] Some observers claim that the junta is heavily involved in both the legal and illegal trade of gemstones, as the regime controls most mining operations and the sale of gems through official auctions and private sales reportedly arranged by senior military officers.[51] Congress has also accused the Burmese regime of attempting to evade U.S. sanctions against the import of Burmese gemstones by concealing the gems' origin from potential buyers.[52] Congress estimates that while 90% of the world's rubies originate from Burma, only 3% of those entering the United States are claimed to have originated there.

Other Contraband

AK-47s, B-40 rocket launchers, and other small arms are reportedly smuggled into Burma along the Thai-Burmese border. These weapons reportedly go to the Karen guerrillas, who continue to fight a decades-long insurgency against the Burmese junta. Another report implicates the Shan State Army in trafficking in military hardware.[53] Although analysts say it is unlikely that the ruling junta benefits from the criminal profits of small arms trafficking, reports indicate that the government distributes such weapons to its cadre of child soldiers.[54] Other less high-profile markets for contraband reportedly exist, including trafficking in cigarettes, cars, CDs, pornography, antiques, religious items, fertilizer, and counterfeit documents—many of which are believed to involve at least the complicity of some Burmese government officials.

In April 2008, Japan's public broadcaster NHK reported that Burma has been importing multiple- launch rockets from North Korea, raising international concerns and speculation about why Burma would seek out such weapons in violation of U.N. sanctions imposed on North Korea after its nuclear test in October 2006.[55] Some observers speculate that the Burmese military has been seeking to upgrade its artillery to improve the country's protection against potential external threats.[56] Burma and North Korea are thought to have been involved in conventional weapons trade in violation of U.N. sanctions since spring 2007, when North Korea and Burma resumed diplomatic relations with each other. Observers further claim that "Western intelligence officials have suspected for several years that the regime has had an interest in following the model of North Korea and achieving military autarky by developing ballistic missiles and nuclear weapons."[57]

Money Laundering

The State Department reports in 2008 that Burma is a money laundering risk because of its underdeveloped financial sector and large volume of informal trade. In 2001, the international Financial Action Task Force on Money Laundering (FATF) designated Burma as a Non- Cooperative Country or Territory (NCCT) for deficient anti-money laundering provisions and weak oversight of its banking sector.[58] A year later in 2002, the U.S. Department of Treasury's Financial Crimes Enforcement Network (FinCEN) issued an advisory to U.S. financial institutions to give enhanced scrutiny to any financial transaction related to Burma.[59] In 2003, two of Burma's largest private banks—Myanmar Mayflower Bank and Asia Wealth Bank—were implicated by FATF as involved in laundering illicit narcotics proceeds and counterfeiting. The Secretary of the Treasury in 2003 listed Burma as a "major money laundering country of primary concern" and in 2004 imposed additional countermeasures.[60] Burma has since revoked the operating licenses of the two banks implicated in 2003. However, the U.S. government and international bodies, such as FATF, continue to monitor the widespread use of informal money transfer networks, sometimes also referred to as "hundi" or "hawala." Monies sent through these informal systems are usually legitimate remittances from relatives abroad. The lack of transparency and regulation of these money transfers remain issues of concern for the United States. In other parts of the world, hawala or hawala-like techniques have been used, or are suspected of being used, to launder proceeds derived from narcotics trafficking, terrorism, alien smuggling, and other criminal activities.[61]

U.S. POLICY

Sanctions and Special Measures

Burma is subject to a broad sanctions regime that addresses issues of U.S. interest, which include democracy, human rights, and international crime.[62] Specifically in response to the extent of transnational crime occurring in Burma, the President has taken additional actions against the country under several different legislative authorities. Burma is listed as a major drug-producing state, and because of its insufficient effort to combat the narcotics trade, the country is barred access to some U.S. foreign assistance.[63] As an uncooperative, major drug-producing state, Burma is also subject to trade sanctions.[64] In 2005, the Department of Justice indicted eight Burmese individuals identified in 2003 by the U.S. Treasury's Office of Foreign Assets Control (OFAC) for their alleged role in drug trafficking and money laundering.[65] On November 13, 2008, OFAC named 26 individuals and 17 companies tied to Burma's Wei Hsueh Kang and the UWSA as Specially Designated Narcotics Traffickers pursuant to the Foreign Narcotics Kingpin Designation Act (21 U.S.C. 1901-1908).[66]

Burma is characterized by the State Department's 2009 Trafficking in Persons report as a Tier 3 state engaged in the most severe forms of trafficking in persons; as such, Burma is subject to sanctions, barring the country from non-humanitarian, non-trade-related U.S. assistance and loss of U.S. support for loans from international financial institutions.[67] As a major money laundering country—defined by Section 481 (e)(7) of the Foreign Assistance Act of 1961, as amended, as one "whose financial institutions engage in currency transactions including significant amounts of proceeds from international narcotics trafficking"—Burma is subject to several "special measures" to regulate and monitor financial flows. These include Department of Treasury advisories for enhanced scrutiny over financial transactions, as well as five special measures listed under 31 U.S.C. 5318A.[68] The United States does not apply sanctions against Burma in specific response to its activity in other illicit trades, including wildlife.[69] The Block Burmese JADE (Junta's Anti-Democratic Efforts) Act of 2007 (H.R. 3890), however, would prohibit the importation of gems and hardwoods from Burma, among other restrictions.[70]

After more than a decade of applying sanctions against Burma, however, many analysts have concluded that the sanctions have done little to change the situation. The effectiveness of U.S. sanctions is limited by several factors.[71] These include (1) unevenly applied sanctions against Burma by other countries and international organizations, including the European Union and Japan; (2) a booming natural gas production and export industry that provides the SPDC with significant revenue; (3) continued unwillingness of Burma's fellow members in the Association of Southeast Asian Nations (ASEAN) to impose economic sanctions against Burma; (4) Burma's historical isolation from the global economy; and (5) China's continued economic and military assistance to Burma. In addition, some analysts suggest that sanctions are, in part, culpable for the flourishing black markets in Burma, including trafficking in humans, gems, and drugs, because legal exports are barred.[72] Several analysts indicate that many Burmese women who lost their jobs in the textile industry as a result of Western sanctions are among the victims of trafficking for sexual exploitation.[73]

Regional Border Control Assistance

The United States is assisting neighboring countries with stemming the flow of trafficked contraband from Burma into their territories. Although most U.S. assistance to combat transnational crime in Burma remains in suspension, the United States is working to train law enforcement and border control officials in neighboring countries through anti-crime assistance programs.[74] Currently, the bulk of funding to Burma's neighbors remains concentrated in counter- narcotics and anti-human trafficking projects; no funding is allocated to the State Department for combating "organized and gang-related crime" in the region. Overall funding to combat trafficking has been in decline for several years; the Administration's FY2008 appropriations request for Foreign

Operations in the region represents a 24.2% decrease from FY2006 actual funding.

Source: Map Resources. Adapted by CRS.

Figure 2. Map of Burma

A New Approach?

Despite Burma's recent progress in reducing opium poppy cultivation, most experts believe U.S. policies have not yielded substantial leverage in combating transnational crime emanating from Burma. In light of the most recent displays of junta violence against political demonstrators in September 2007, however, there are indications of increasing political interest in re-evaluating U.S. policy toward Burma. Among the considerations that policy makers have recently raised are (1) whether the United States should increase the amount of humanitarian aid sent to Burma; (2) what role ASEAN and other multilateral vehicles for dialogue could play in increasing political pressure on the junta regime; (3) what role the United States sees India, as the world's largest democracy and Burma's neighbor, playing in ensuring that Burma does not become a source of regional instability; and (4) how the United States can further work with China and Thailand, as the largest destinations of trafficked goods from Burma, to address transnational crime along Burma's borders.

End Notes

[1] See discussion on "Official Corruption."
[2] For example, the 2006 *National Security Strategy of the United States* (at http://www.whitehouse.gov/nsc/nss.html*)* identifies addressing ungoverned areas as among U.S. national security priorities because of concern that they could be used as safe havens for terrorists. See also Angel Rabasa et al., *Ungoverned Territories: Understanding and Reducing Terrorism Risks* (Santa Monica, CA: Rand Corporation, 2007).
[3] Laws under which drug-related sanctions are authorized include Section 489(a)(1) of the Foreign Assistance Act of 1961 (P.L. 87-195), as amended (22 U.S.C. 2291j(a)(1)); the Narcotics Control Trade Act (P.L. 99-570), as amended (19 U.S.C. 2491 et seq.); and Section 138 of Title I, Subtitle D, of the Customs and Trade Act of 1990 (P.L. 101-382).
[4] Pursuant to the Victims of Trafficking and Violence Protection Act of 2000 (P.L. 106-386), as amended.
[5] U.S. Department of State, *International Narcotics Control Strategy Report*, vol. 1 (2008).
[6] Jane's Sentinel Security Assessment: Southeast Asia, April 30, 2008; Antonio Nicaso and Lee Lamothe, *Angels, Mobsters, and Narco-Terrorists: The Rising Menace of Global Criminal Enterprises* (Ontario, Canada: John Wiley & Sons, 2005).
[7] Economist Intelligence Unit, *Myanmar (Burma) Country Profile* (2006).
[8] U.S. Department of State, *International Narcotics Control Strategy Report*, vols. 1 and 2 (2008); Jane's Sentinel Security Assessment: Southeast Asia, April 30, 2008, *op cit.*; Economist Intelligence Unit, *op cit.*; Transparency International, *Corruption Perceptions Index* (2007). According to some analysts, corruption among police and border patrol officials in Burma's neighboring countries also eases the flow of trafficked goods out of Burma. See also Nora Boustany, "Burmese Activist Urges Stronger U.S. Sanctions," *The Washington Post*, November 2, 2007. In this news article, Maung Maung, secretary general of the National Council of the Union of Burma, stated that "the country's revenue from gas, rubies, teak, timber, rice, gas, uranium, and diamonds is being pilfered for the personal enrichment of junta members or their families."
[9] Transparency International, *Corruption Perceptions Index* (2009).
[10] 2008 *International Narcotics Control Strategy Report*, vol. 1, *op cit.*
[11] Michael Black and Anthony Davis, "Wa and Peace: The UWSA and Tensions in Myanmar," *Jane's Intelligence Review*, March 2008.

[12] 2008 *International Narcotics Control Strategy Report*, vol. 1, *op cit.*
[13] See CRS Report RL33479, *Burma-U.S. Relations*, by Larry A. Niksch; Christopher S. Wren, "Road to Riches Starts in the Golden Triangle," *New York Times*, May 5, 1998; Robert S. Gelbard, "Slorc's Drug Links," *Far Eastern Economic Review*, November 21, 1996; Anthony Davis, "The Wa Challenge Regional Stability in Southeast Asia," *Jane's Intelligence Review*, January 2003.
[14] "Imposition of Special Measures against Burma as a Jurisdiction of Primary Money Laundering Concern," *Federal Register*, Vol. 68, No. 227, November 25, 2003.
[15] See for example Colin Freeman, "Burmese Drug Lord Lands Lucrative Reconstruction Contracts," *Edmonton Journal* (Alberta), May 25, 2008.
[16] U.S. Department of the Treasury, "Treasury Sanctions Additional Financial Operatives of the Burmese Regime," Press Release, February 25, 2008; U.S. Department of the Treasury, "Steven Law Financial Network," Report, February 2008; and "Key Financial Operatives of the Burmese Regime Designated by OFAC," World-Check, March 3, 2008.
[17] See United Nations Office on Drugs and Crime (UNODC), *World Drug Report* (2008); 2008 *International Narcotics Control Strategy Report, op cit.*; Global Witness, *A Choice for China: Ending the Destruction of Burma's Northern Frontier Forests* (2005); Jolene Lin, "Tackling Southeast Asia's Illegal Wildlife Trade," *Singapore Year Book of International Law*, vol. 9 (2005); and U.S. Department of State, *Trafficking in Persons Report* (2007).
[18] U.S. Drug Enforcement Administration, "Methamphetamine: The Current Threat in East Asia and the Pacific Rim," *Drug Intelligence Brief*, September 2003.
[19] U.S. Fish and Wildlife Service, Annual Report FY2006, August 2007; "Wildlife Smuggling Boom Plaguing L.A., Authorities Say," *National Geographic News*, July 26, 2007.
[20] Michael Lyman, *Organized Crime* (Upper Saddle River, NJ: Prentice Hall, 2007).
[21] 2007 *Trafficking in Persons Report, op cit.*
[22] Association of Southeast Asian Nations (ASEAN), "Cooperation on Drugs and Narcotics: Overview," at http://www.aseansec.org/5682.htm; 2008 *International Narcotics Control Strategy Report*, vol. 1, *op cit.*
[23] This annual list is required by section 706(1) of the Foreign Relations Authorization Act, Fiscal Year 2003 (P.L. 107-228).
[24] The "Golden Triangle" refers to an area of approximately 135,000 square miles of mountains that surround the Burma-Laos-Thailand border region. In the 1980s and 1990s, the Golden Triangle reigned as the world's largest producer of opium poppy.
[25] Jane's Sentinel Security Assessment: Southeast Asia, April 30, 2008, *op cit.* Note, however, that not all cease-fire groups are involved in the illegal drug trade.
[26] See for example, "U.S. Department of State, "Urging an End to the Violence in Eastern Burma," August 31, 2009.
[27] Thomas Fuller, "Crackdown Spurs a Heroin Clearance Sale in Southeast Asia," *New York Times*, October 1, 2009.
[28] See for example, "Thai PM Launches New 'War on Drugs,'" *Agence France Presse*, March 19, 2008; Brian McCartan, "Despite Strong Rhetoric, Thailand's Latest Drug War a Restrained Campaign," *World Politics Review*, May 2008; Daniel Ten Kate, "Thailand to Restart War on Drugs," *Asia Sentinel*, March 2008.
[29] U.S. Drug Enforcement Administration, *Drugs of Abuse*, 2005, available at http://www.usdoj.gov/dea/pubs/abuse doa-p.pdf.
[30] See for example testimony by Vanda Felbab Brown, "Threats from Transnational Drug Enterprises," House Oversight and Government Reform Committee, Subcommittee on National Security and Foreign Affairs, October 1, 2009.
[31] Tor Norling, "Haven or Hell," *The Irrawaddy*, July 11, 2008.
[32] UNODC, *World Drug Report* (2009); see also: Jane's Sentinel Security Assessment: Southeast Asia, April 30, 2008, *op cit.*
[33] UNODC, *Opium Poppy Cultivation in South-East Asia: Lao PDR, Myanmar* (December 2009).

[34] Black and Davis, *op cit.* See also: Central Intelligence Agency, *World Factbook* (2007); 2008 *International Narcotics Control Strategy Report*, vol. 1, *op cit.*

[35] Ibid.

[36] U.S. Department of State, 2008 *International Narcotics Control Strategy Report*, vol. 1, *op cit.*; Jane's Sentinel Security Assessment: Southeast Asia, April 30, 2008, *op cit.*; and David Johnson, Assistant Secretary of State for International Narcotics and Law Enforcement Affairs, News Briefing, February 29, 2008.

[37] Jane's Sentinel Security Assessment: Southeast Asia, April 30, 2008, *op cit.*

[38] U.S. Department of State, 2008 *International Narcotics Control Strategy Report*, vol. 1, *op cit.*

[39] Ibid.

[40] "Intelligence: Drug Scam Suspected," *The Irrawaddy*, July 2008.

[41] 2009 *Trafficking in Persons Report*; Sold to Be Soldiers: Human Rights Watch, *The Recruitment and Use of Child Soldiers in Burma*, October 2007. See also "Burma/Myanmar: After the Crackdown," *International Crisis Group*, Asia Report No. 144, January 31, 2008.

[42] 2007 *Trafficking in Persons Report*, p. 71.

[43] Kocha Olarn, "Myanmar Migrant Survivors Fined and Deported," *CNN*, April 12, 2008.

[44] The sectors included bamboo; green, soy, and yellow beans; bricks; jade; palm thatch; physic nuts/castor beans; rice; rubber; rubies; sesame; shrimp; sugarcane; sunflowers; and teak. See U.S. Department of Labor, *The Department of Labor's List of Goods Produced by Child Labor or Forced Labor*, September 10, 2009.

[45] Global Witness (2005), *op cit.*

[46] See, for example, Vaudine England, "The Mekong Connection in Illegal Log Trade," *Sunday Morning Post* (Hong Kong), March 23, 2008.

[47] Christopher Shepherd and Vincent Nijman, "An Assessment of Wildlife Trade at Mong La Market on the MyanmarChina Border," *TRAFFIC Bulletin*, vol. 21, no. 2 (2007).

[48] "Factbox: Why Are Asia's Endangered Animals So Sought After?" *Reuters News*, September 3, 2007.

[49] Lin, *op cit.*

[50] "Myanmar Rubies, Sapphires for Sale at Gems Fairs," *Reuters News*, October 19, 2006.

[51] See "Burma: Gem Trade Bolsters Military Regime, Fuels Atrocities," *Human Rights Watch*, November 12, 2007; "Burma and Blood Gems," Leber Jeweler, Inc., available at http://www.leberjeweler.com/stones/ burma_bloodgems.php3.

[52] See P.L. 108-61; U.S. House of Representatives, Block Burmese JADE (Junta's Anti-Democratic Efforts) Act of 2007, H.Rept. 110-418, Part 1, October 31, 2007.

[53] Eric Tagliacozzo, "Border Permeability and the State in Southeast Asia: Contraband and Regional Security," *Contemporary Southeast Asia*, vol. 23, no. 2 (2001).

[54] Human Rights Watch, *Small Arms and Human Rights: The Need for Global Action; A Human Rights Watch Briefing Paper for the U.N. Biennial Meeting on Small Arms* (2003).

[55] "N. Korea Exporting Multiple-Launch Rockets to Myanmar—Report," *CNBC*, April 2, 2008; "North Korea Sells Rocket Launchers to Myanmar—Report," *Reuters News*, April 3, 2008; and U.N. Security Council Resolution 1718 (2006).

[56] See for example "Oslo-Based Website: Burma's Purchase of North Korean Arms Threatens Stability," *BBC Monitoring Asia Pacific*, April 6, 2008; "Thai-Based Website: U.S. Concerned over Reports of North Korean Weapons to Burma," *BBC Monitoring Asia Pacific*, April 6, 2008.

[57] Michael Green and Derek Mitchell, "Asia's Forgotten Crisis: A New Approach to Burma," *Foreign Affairs*, November/December 2007, Vol. 86, Issue 6.

[58] Created in 1989, the Financial Action Task Force (FATF) is an inter-governmental body whose purpose is the development and promotion of national and international policies to combat money laundering and terrorist financing.

[59] See 31 CFR Part 103, Department of the Treasury, Financial Crimes Enforcement Network, Imposition of Special Measures against Burma.

[60] Pursuant to 31 U.S.C. 531 8A, as added by Section 311 of the USA PATRIOT Act (P.L. 107-56), these countermeasures prohibited U.S. banks from establishing or maintaining correspondent or payable-through accounts in the United States for or on behalf of Myanmar Mayflower and Asia Wealth Bank and, with narrow exceptions, for all other Burmese banks. See 2007 *International Narcotics Control Strategy Report*, vol. 2, *op cit.*

[61] Patrick M. Jost and Harjit S. Sandhu, *The Hawala Alternative Remittance System and its Role in Money Laundering* (Lyon, France: Interpol General Secretariat, 2000).

[62] Notable sanctions among those not specifically related to international crime include the Burmese Freedom and Democracy Act of 2003 (P.L. 108-61, extended by P.L. 108-272 and P.L. 109-39); Executive Order 13047, issued May 20, 1997, under Section 570 of the Foreign Appropriations Act, 1997 (P.L. 104-208); and Executive Order 13310, issued July 28, 2003, to implement P.L. 108-6 1 (the President announced additional modifications September 25 and 27, 2007). See also CRS Report RS22737, *Burma: Economic Sanctions*, by Larry A. Niksch and Martin A. Weiss.

[63] Pursuant to Section 489(a)(1) of the Foreign Assistance Act of 1961, as amended.

[64] Trade sanctions are pursuant to the Narcotics Control Trade Act (19 U.S.C. 249 1-2495) and the Customs and Trade Act of 1990 (P.L. 101-382).

[65] The indictments were made using the Foreign Narcotics Kingpin Designation Act (21 U.S.C. 1901-1908). The indicted Burmese have yet to be arrested or brought to trial in the United States.

[66] U.S. Department of State, International Narcotics Control Strategy Report, Vol. 2, March 2009. Kang was designated by the President as a Foreign Narcotics Kingpin on June 1, 2000, and the UWSA on June 2, 2003.

[67] Sanctions are pursuant to the Victims of Trafficking and Violence Protection Act of 2000 (P.L. 106-386). The decision to apply sanctions under P.L. 106-3 86 is left to presidential discretion.

[68] These include (1) record-keeping and reporting of certain financial transactions, (2) collection of information relating to beneficial ownership, (3) collection of information relating to certain payable-through accounts, (4) collection of information relating to certain correspondent accounts, and (5) prohibition or conditions on the opening or maintaining of correspondent or payable-through accounts for a foreign financial institution. See Douglas N. Greenburg, John Roth, and Katherine A. Sawyer, "Special Measures under Section 311 of the USA PATRIOT Act," *The Review of Banking and Financial Services*, vol. 23, no. 6, June 2007.

[69] Notably, President Bill Clinton in 1994 used the 1971 Pelly Amendment to the Fishermen's Protective Act of 1967, as amended (22 U.S.C. 1978), as a means by which to impose sanctions against Taiwan for its alleged insufficient progress toward eliminating the country's illegal trade in rhino and tiger parts and products. The sanction temporarily banned the importation of certain fish and wildlife products from Taiwan.

[70] Last major action to H.R. 3890: passed Senate with an amendment and an amendment to the Title on December 19, 2007.

[71] See CRS Report RL33479, *Burma-U.S. Relations, op cit.*

[72] Fareed Zakaria, "Sleepwalking to Sanctions, Again," *Newsweek*, October 15, 2007.

[73] See, for example, "U.S. Sanctions 'Hit Burma Hard,'" *BBC News*, October 3, 2003.

[74] Under authorities granted in Section 2291 of the Foreign Assistance Act of 1961, as amended, the State Department is responsible for coordinating foreign assistance and law enforcement training for counter-narcotics and anti-crime programming. According to the Administration's FY2008 Foreign Operations Budget Justification, such programs exist in four of Burma's neighbors: Thailand, Laos, India, and Bangladesh.

In: Bangladesh and Burma: Background and Issues ISBN: 978-1-61761-219-0
Editor: Brandon E. Stromberg   © 2011 Nova Science Publishers, Inc.

Chapter 5

BURMA: ECONOMIC SANCTIONS

Larry A. Niksch and Martin A. Weiss

SUMMARY

On October 19, 2007, President George W. Bush issued Executive Order 13449. This followed a September 25, 2007 statement by President Bush that sanctions against Burma, which have been in place since 1997, would be tightened to specifically target leading Burmese officials and impose additional financial and travel sanctions. This chapter provides background information on existing economic sanctions against Burma and possible options to expand sanctions.

The following table provides summary information on existing Burma sanctions.

Table 1. Summary of U.S. Economic Sanctions on Burma

Statutory Action	Sanction	Exemption
Executive Order 13047, May 20, 1997. Issued un-der Section 570 of the Foreign	Prohibits new investment in Burma by U.S. persons and companies on or after May 21, 1997. New investment is defined as a contract with the Government of Burma or a	Companies with invest-ments in Burma prior to May 21, 1997, and companies or persons with an investment agreement in place prior to

Table 1. (Continued)

Statutory Action	Sanction	Exemption
Appropriations Act, 1997 (P.L. 104-208)	non-governmental entity in Burma for the development of resources located in Burma, purchasing a share of ownership in a project, or entering into an agreement that provides for a participation in royalties, earnings, or profits from the economic development of resources located in Burma.	May 21, 1997. The exemption in-cludes the U.S. corporation UNOCAL and its investment with the French corporation Total in natural gas exploration and pipeline offshore and across Burma into Thailand. It is estimated that the project provides $400 million to $647 million to the Burmese government annually. (Seekins, Donald M. "Burma and U.S. Sanctions: Punishing an Authoritarian Regime." Asian Survey, May-June 2005. p. 452.)
P.L. 108-61, Burmese Freedom and Democracy Act of 2003, July 28, 2003. Exten-ded by P.L. 108-272 and P.L. 109-39.	Requires the President to ban the importation into the United States of certain products of Burma, beginning 30 days after the date of enactment. The import ban expires in one year unless renewed. The President may impose a freeze on funds or assets in the United States of the Burmese Government and individuals who hold senior positions in that government. Requires the U.S. government to vote against the extension of any financial assistance to Burma by international financial institutions. Authorizes the President to deny visas and entry into the United States to former and present leaders of the Burmese government or the Union Solidarity Development Association (a pro-government mass organization).	The President may wai-ve the prohibition on the import of any product from Burma if the President determines and notifies the appropriate congressional committees that to do so "is in the national interest of the United States."
Executive Order 13310, July 28, 2003.	Issued to implement P.L. 108-61. Blocks property and property interests of persons listed in the Annex to the Executive Order and persons designated by the Treasury Department as being senior officials of the Government of Burma and the Union Solidarity and Development Association. Authorizes the Treasury to designate individuals or entities that are owned or controlled by, or acting on behalf of any of those officeals or groups. Bans the importation into the United States of products of Burma and the export or	Transactions prior to May 21, 1997, between a U.S. person or company and any entity in Burma, but such transactions with banks in Burma must be conducted through a non-U.S. bank. No prohibition on the export of goods and services other than financial services. Exemption for transfer of personal remittances of less than $300 to and from Burma for "an individual ordinarily resident in Burma, provided that the funds are not

Table 1. (Continued)

Statutory Action	Sanction	Exemption
	re-export of financial services to Burma by U.S. persons. Prohibits a U.S. person or company from approving, aiding, or supporting a foreign party's investment in Burma. Prohibits U.S. persons from purchasing shares in a third-country company if the company's profits are predominantly derived from the company's development of resources in Burma.	being sent by, to or on behalf of a blocked party." The U.S. Office of Foreign Assets Control can issue licenses to non-government organizations to engage in humanitarian or religious activities in Burma.
Executive Order 13448, October 19, 2007.	Grants the Treasury Department expanded authority to designate for sanctions individuals responsible for human rights abuses as well as public corruption, and those who provide material and financial backing to these individuals or to the government of Burma.	
Section 489(a)(1) of the Foreign Assistance Act of 1961, as amended.	Burma is listed by the Department of State as a "major illicit drug producing country" and is subsequently barred from receiving some U.S. foreign assistance.	
Narcotics Control Trade Act (19 U.S.C. 2491-2495) and the Customs and Trade Act of 1990 (P.L. 101-382).	Due to its designation as a major drug producing state, Burma is subject to several trade sanctions including: (1) deny to any or all of the products of that country tariff treatment under the Generalized System of Preferences, the Caribbean Basin Economic Recovery Act [19 U.S.C. 2701 et seq.], or any other law providing preferential tariff treatment; (2) apply to any or all of the dutiable products of that country an additional duty at a rate not to exceed 50 percent ad valorem or the specific rate equivalent; (3) apply to one or more duty-free products of that country a duty at a rate not to exceed 50 percent ad valorem; (4) take the steps described in subsection (d)(1) or (d)(2) of this section, or both, to curtail air transportation between the United States and that country; and/or withdraw the personnel and resources of the United States from participation in any arrangement with that country for the pre-clearance of customs by visitors	

Table 1. (Continued)

Statutory Action	Sanction	Exemption
	between the United States and that country.	
Executive Order 13464, April 30, 2008.	Froze assets in the United States and prohibited U.S. firms from doing business with three Burmese companies: Myanmar Pearl Enterprise, Myanmar Gem Enterprise, and Myanmar Timber Enterprise.	
P.L. 110-286, Tom Lantos Burmese JADE Act of 2008, July 29, 2008	Bans the import of jadeite and rubies mined in Burma and jewelry containing jadeite or rubies made in Burma. Exporters of jadeite, rubies, and jewelry from other countries to the United States must act to prohibit inclusion of articles from Burma; must maintain full records of non-Burmese articles and controls from mine to final finishing to export. Governments must establish "dissuasive penalties" against persons who violate laws and regulations against trade in Burmese-origin articles. The President shall appoint a Special Representative and Policy Coord-inator for Burma. The State Department shall submit to Congress reports on countries and entities that supply arms and intelligence aid to the Burmese government; and countries and foreign banks that hold assets of senior Burmese officials. The Act expresses the "sense of Congress" that the investors in the Yadana natural gas project (including the U.S. firm, Chevron) should "consider voluntary divestment over time" if the Burmese government fails to reform politically; and the investors should publicly disclose their role in the investment and the amount of financial support to the Burmese government generated by the Yadana project.	
P.L. 111-42	Renewed P.L. 108-61, The Burmese Freedom and Democracy Act of 2003.	

Source: Compiled by the Congressional Research Service.

FUTURE OPTIONS TO EXPAND SANCTIONS

In response to the Burmese government's suppression of demonstrations at the end of September 2007, the Bush Administration published a large number of names of persons and companies connected with the Burmese government, imposed bans on their travel to the United States, and froze their financial assets in the United States. Existing sanctions against Burma may be viewed as adequate and as necessitating no further action. However, Members of the 111th Congress may seek to exercise additional options. P.L. 110-286, the Tom Lantos Block Burmese JADE Act of 2008 struck provisions in the House version of the bill that would have prohibited "United States persons" from entering into economic-financial transactions, paying taxes, or performing "any contract" with Burmese government institutions or individuals under U.S. sanctions. The prohibition of the payment of taxes specifically included the payments of taxes to the Burmese government by the Yadana natural gas project, in which the U.S. corporation, Chevron, is a major partner. These stricken provisions were replaced in the final bill by a "sense of Congress" statement that Chevron and the other foreign investors should consider voluntary disinvestment from the project. Other options to expand sanctions include the following.

Impose provisions of the USA PATRIOT Act on third country banks and financial institutions that do business with Burmese banks and individuals associated with the Government of Burma: Under Section 311 of the USA PATRIOT Act, *Special Measures for Jurisdictions, Financial Institutions, or International Transactions of Primary Money Laundering Concern*, the Secretary of the Treasury is authorized to impose any of five certain regulatory restrictions, known as "special measures."[1] These can be used upon finding that a foreign jurisdiction, financial institution, or certain transactions or accounts is "of primary money laundering concern." Prior to making such a finding, the Treasury Secretary must consult with the Secretary of State and the Attorney General and consider certain factors relating to the foreign jurisdiction or the particular institution targeted. Among the factors to be considered are: involvement with organized crime or terrorists, bank secrecy laws and regulations, the existence of a mutual legal assistance treaty with the United States, and level of official corruption.

Of the five types of special measures, four of the five impose information-gathering and record-keeping requirements on U.S. financial institutions dealing either directly with the jurisdiction designated as one of primary money laundering concern, or dealing with those having direct dealings with the designated jurisdiction. Under the fifth special measure, a U.S. financial institution may be prohibited from opening or maintaining in the United States a correspondent or payable-through account[2] for a foreign financial institution if the account involves the designee.

On November 18, 2003, the Secretary of the Treasury designated Burma as a jurisdiction of primary money laundering concern and applied a "special measure" under Section 311 of the USA PATRIOT Act. The special measure prohibits covered U.S. financial institutions from establishing, maintaining, administering, or managing in the United States any correspondent or payable-through account for, or on behalf of, a Burmese banking institution. Covered U.S. financial institutions also are similarly prohibited with regard to any correspondent or payable- through account in the United States for any foreign bank if the account is used by the foreign bank to provide banking services to a Burmese banking institution. However, the special measure applied to Burmese banks does not prohibit U.S. financial institutions from maintaining correspondent accounts otherwise prohibited by this rule if such accounts are permitted to be maintained pursuant to Executive Order 13310 and the Burma-related activity of those accounts is solely for the purposing of conducting exempted activity. This is in contrast to the Treasury Department's imposition of Section 311 on Banco Delta Asia in the Chinese territory of Macau for money laundering for North Korea. Section 311 measures have arguably had their largest success in this designation of Macau-based Banco Delta Asia in September 2005 and the full imposition of Section 311 in March 2007. The North Korean government had used Banco Delta for the majority of its international transactions. Reportedly, following the U.S. proposed designation, over two dozen financial institutions ceased their transactions with North Korea.[3] Most importantly, China froze North Korean accounts in the Macau branch of the Bank of China and reportedly cracked down on North Korean efforts to circulate counterfeit U.S. dollars in China near the North Korean border.[4]

Reports of third country banks that do business with Burmese banks or individuals connected to the Burmese government (including drug traffickers) are sparse. Past reports have cited banks in Thailand, Singapore, and China. Burmese accounts in Chinese banks were confirmed in January 2006 when the Bank of China ordered Chinese banks to terminate all U.S. dollar business with the Myanmar Foreign Trade Bank and the Myanmar Investment and Commercial Bank.[5]

End Notes

[1] For more information on Title III of the USA PATRIOT Act, see CRS Report RL3 1208, *International Money Laundering Abatement and Anti-Terrorist Financing Act of 2001, Title III of P.L. 107-56 (USA PATRIOT Act),* by M. Maureen Murphy.

[2] A payable-through account is an account established at a U.S. financial institution that extends check-writing privileges to the customers of other, often foreign, financial institutions.

[3] "Press reports indicate that some two dozen financial institutions across the globe have voluntarily cut back or terminated their business with North Korea, notably including institutions in China, Japan, Vietnam, Mongolia, and Singapore. The result of these voluntary actions is that it is becoming very difficult for the Kim Jong-Il regime to benefit from its criminal conduct." Testimony of Daniel Glaser, Deputy Assistant Secretary for Terrorist Financing and Financial Crimes, U.S. Department of the Treasury before the Senate Committee on Banking, Housing, and Urban Affairs. September 12, 2006.

[4] Ibid.

[5] Turnell, Sean. Burma's Economic Prospects. Testimony before the Subcommittee on East Asian and Pacific Affairs, Senate Foreign Relations Committee, March 29, 2006. Sweeney, John. "How Junta protects Mr. Heroin." The Observer (London, internet version), April 8, 2001. Casanier, Francois. "A Narco-dictatorship in progress." BurmaNet News, June 13, 1996.

In: Bangladesh and Burma: Background and Issues ISBN: 978-1-61761-219-0
Editor: Brandon E. Stromberg   © 2011 Nova Science Publishers, Inc.

Chapter 6

STATEMENT OF SENATOR RICHARD G. LUGAR, EAST ASIAN AND PACIFIC AFFAIRS SUBCOMMITTEE OF THE FOREIGN RELATIONS COMMITTEE

Thank you, Chairman Webb for holding this hearing to review U.S. policy toward Burma, and I also extend appreciation to Senator Inhofe for his work as Ranking Member on the East Asian and Pacific Affairs Subcommittee.

This hearing is timely given the Obama Administration's review of the United States' policy on Burma.

As the United States contemplates policy options, we will, I hope, compare notes with other countries actively engaged in Burma. China, Japan, India, Thailand, Singapore and South Korea are among those nations who are direct witness to the deteriorating education and healthcare infrastructure within Burma. The mismanagement of Burma's economy started long before imposition of U.S. sanctions.

At a massive cost to themselves and the United Nations, Thailand and Malaysia receive hundreds of thousands of migrants and refugees, largely ethnic minorities, who continue to flee Burma. More than 50,000 persons have now applied through UNHCR offices in Malaysia and Thailand for resettlement to a third country. Ten thousand Burmese refugees have now resettled in my home state of Indiana.

The Obama Administration's policy review includes reference to the growing North Korea – Burma relationship. The United States has a responsibility to our friends and allies throughout Asia to oppose actively the possible proliferation of weapons of mass destruction to or from Burma. Since I first discussed the troubling prospects of renewed ties between these two countries in 2004, the Foreign Relations Committee has repeatedly raised the issue of Burma's growing relationship with North Korea with a wide array of U.S. Administration officials.

For example, we have questioned the basis for hundreds of Burmese officials going to Russia for technical education which included nuclear technology training. The number of persons travelling to Russia for specialized training seemed to be far beyond the number needed for the eventual operation of a nuclear reactor for medical research purposes, intended to be built by the junta with Russian government assistance.

Burma's multiple uranium deposits, reports of uranium refining and processing plants, and it's active nuclear program reportedly assisted by North Korea collectively point to reason for concern in a country whose officials resist transparency.

Dr. Sigfried Hecker, Director Emeritus of Los Alamos National Laboratory and now Co-Director of the Center for International Security and Cooperation at Stanford University recently wrote, "The A.Q. Khan network connected companies, individuals and front organizations into a dangerous proliferation ring. The revelations of the North Korean reactor in Syria, along with developments in Iran and Burma, appear to point toward a different type of proliferation ring --- one run by national governments, perhaps also assisted by other clandestine networks".

Mr. Chairman, today's witnesses represent distinguished experts on Burma. I am pleased to introduce a Hoosier, Professor David Williams, Executive Director of the Center for Constitutional Democracy at Indiana University, who has extensive background on Burma-related issues. Again, Mr. Chairman, thank you for holding today's hearing.

In: Bangladesh and Burma: Background and Issues ISBN: 978-1-61761-219-0
Editor: Brandon E. Stromberg © 2011 Nova Science Publishers, Inc.

Chapter 7

TESTIMONY OF KURT CAMPBELL, ASSISTANT SECRETARY OF STATE, BUREAU OF EAST ASIAN AND PACIFIC AFFAIRS, BEFORE THE SUBCOMMITTEE ON EAST ASIAN AND PACIFIC AFFAIRS, HEARING ON "U.S. POLICY TOWARD BURMA"

Mr. Chairman, Senator Inhofe, and Members of the Subcommittee, thank you for inviting me here today to testify about U.S. policy toward Burma and a possible new direction for U.S.-Burma relations.

Let me take this opportunity to brief you on the overarching assessments that helped shape our review. The Administration launched a review of our Burma policy seven months ago, recognizing that political and humanitarian conditions in Burma were deplorable. Neither sanctions nor engagement, implemented alone, have succeeded in improving those conditions and moving Burma forward on a path to democratic reform.

Moreover, it was clear to us that the problems Burma presents, not only to its people, but to its neighbors, the wider region and the world at large, demand that we review and reconsider our approach. In addition to taking a hard look at the current situation inside Burma, we also focused on emerging questions and concerns regarding Burma's relationship with North Korea, particularly in light of the passage of UN Security Council Resolution 1874, which prohibits member states from engaging in trade with North Korea in virtually all conventional weapons as well as in sensitive technologies, including those related to ballistic missiles and nuclear and other WMD programs.

Our policy review also was informed by the fact that, for the first time in recent memory, the Burmese leadership has shown an active interest in engaging with the United States. But, let me be clear: we have decided to engage with Burma because we believe it is in our interest to do so.

We have consulted widely throughout the review process with Congress, other governments, and key stakeholders such as non-governmental organizations, business leaders, academics, and representatives of international organizations. We also have consulted with the National League for Democracy and other democratic activists inside Burma.

The conclusions of our policy review, just announced this week, reaffirmed our fundamental interests in Burma: we support a unified, peaceful, prosperous, and democratic Burma. While our goals in Burma remain the same as before, the policy review confirmed that we need additional tools to augment those that we have been using in pursuit of our objectives. A policy of pragmatic engagement with the Burmese authorities holds the best hope for advancing our goals. A central element of this approach is a direct, senior-level dialogue with representatives of the Burmese leadership. As the Secretary previewed in her remarks to the Friends of Burma last week, we hope a dialogue with the Burmese regime will lay out a path forward towards change in Burma and a better, more productive bilateral relationship.

Through a direct dialogue, we will be able to test the intentions of the Burmese leadership and the sincerity of their expressed interest in a more positive relationship with the United States. The way forward will be clearly tied to concrete actions on the part of the Burmese leadership addressing our core concerns, particularly in the areas of democracy and human rights.

We will also discuss our proliferation concerns and Burma's close military relationship with North Korea. Burma has said it is committed to comply fully with UN Security Council Resolutions 1718 and 1874. Nevertheless, we remain concerned about the nature and extent of Burma's ties with North Korea. Full and transparent implementation of these resolutions is critical to global peace and security, and we will be looking to the Burmese authorities to deliver on their commitments.

We expect engagement with Burma to be a long, slow, and step-by-step process. We will not judge the success of our efforts at pragmatic engagement by the results of a handful of meetings. Engagement for its own sake is obviously not a goal for U.S. policy, but we recognize that achieving meaningful change in Burma will take time.

We will work to ensure that the Burmese leaders have an absolutely clear understanding of our goals for this dialogue and the core issues on our agenda. A fundamentally different U.S.-Burma relationship will require real progress on democracy and human rights. We will continue to press for the unconditional release of Aung San Suu Kyi and all political prisoners; an end to conflicts with ethnic minority groups; accountability of those responsible for human rights violations; and the initiation of a genuine dialogue among the Burmese government, the democratic opposition, and the ethnic minorities on a shared vision for the way forward in Burma. This last issue is critical, since only the Burmese people themselves can determine the future of their country. Our intent is to use our dialogue with the Burmese authorities to facilitate that process. Only if the government of Burma makes progress toward these goals will it be possible to improve our bilateral relationship in a step-by-step process.

In parallel to the dialogue on our core democracy, human rights and nonproliferation concerns, we hope to identity some initial positive steps the Burmese could take in other areas that would help build momentum in the talks and could potentially allow the United States to respond in an appropriate manner. There are a number of areas in which we might be able improve cooperation to our mutual benefit, such as counter-narcotics, health, environmental protection, and the recovery of World War II-era Missing-in-Action remains.

Our dialogue with Burma will supplement rather than replace the sanctions regime that has been at the center of our Burma policy for many years. Lifting or easing sanctions at the outset of a dialogue without meaningful progress on our concerns would be a mistake. We will maintain our existing sanctions until we see concrete progress, and continue to work with the international community to ensure that those sanctions are effectively coordinated. We believe any easing of sanctions now would send the wrong signal to those who have been striving for so many years for democracy in Burma, to our partners in the region and elsewhere, and to the Burmese leadership itself. Through our dialogue, we also will make clear to the Burmese leadership that relations with the United States can only be improved in a step-by-step process if the Burmese government takes meaningful actions that address our core concerns. Moreover, we will reserve the option of tightening sanctions on the regime and its supporters to respond to events in Burma.

Some argue that sanctions should be lifted immediately because they hurt the people of Burma without effectively pressuring the regime. U.S. sanctions, implemented after the crackdown that began in September 2007, have been "targeted" – aimed not at the people of Burma but at the military leadership, its networks and state-owned companies, and the wealthy cronies that support the government often through illicit activities. It is also important to keep in mind the nature of the country's economic system. Decades of economic mismanagement by Burma's military leadership have resulted in high inflation, endemic corruption, and poor regulation, which have stifled broad-based economic growth. Burma had an unfriendly business environment well before the imposition of sanctions by the United States, the European Union, Canada, and others. The country will continue to be an inhospitable place to invest unless the government introduces serious reforms, rule of law, and good governance. We believe that opening up Burma to the outside world can benefit the forces of change working for a better future for the people of this troubled country.

Our commitment to the Burmese people is unwavering. We will continue to address the urgent humanitarian needs of the population by expanding our assistance efforts in a manner designed to help those most in need without bolstering the regime. We know it can be done. In the wake of Cyclone Nargis, the U.S. Government provided nearly $75 million in aid to the victims of the cyclone through responsible and effective international NGO partners. We also have broadly licensed financial support of not-for-profit humanitarian activities in Burma, and continue to take care to ensure that U.S. sanctions do not impede humanitarian activities by NGOs.

Regarding the elections that the Burmese regime plans to hold in 2010, we need to assess the conditions under which the elections will be held and determine whether opposition and ethnic groups will be able to participate fully. We do not yet know the date of the elections; the authorities also have not published the election laws. Given the way in which the Burmese government conducted its referendum on a new Constitution in the immediate aftermath of Cyclone Nargis, we are skeptical that the elections will be either free or fair. We will continue to stress to the Burmese authorities the baseline conditions that we consider necessary for any credible electoral process. They include the release of political prisoners, the ability of all stakeholders to stand for election, eliminating restrictions on media, and ensuring a free and open campaign.

We will emphasize, and ask that others do the same, that the 2010 elections will only bring legitimacy and stability to the country to the extent that they are broad-based and include all key stakeholders. This is why it is crucial for the regime to begin an internal dialogue now with democratic opposition leaders and representatives of the ethnic minorities. It is only through dialogue that the conditions can be established for all of Burma's political forces to participate. We also intend to remain engaged with the democratic opposition to ensure that our engagement with the regime is not at cross purposes with their own objectives.

We recognize that we alone cannot promote change in Burma. We will need to work with friends and partners to achieve our goals, including stepped up dialogue and interactions with countries such as China and India that have traditionally close relationships with Burma's military leaders. We will continue to coordinate closely as well with ASEAN, the EU, Australia, Canada, Japan, and other actors such as the UN to reinforce our fundamental message on reform to the Burmese regime. We will work with our partners to encourage Burma to be more open and to promote new thinking and new ideas.

Although we hope to initiate these efforts immediately, we are realistic about our expectations. We must be prepared to sustain our efforts beyond the planned 2010 elections. Some day a new generation of leaders in Burma will come to power. If the country is more open to the outside world we can hope to influence that transition and encourage Burma's leaders to take a more positive, constructive, and inclusive path. The process of dialogue itself should give us greater insight into the thinking of Burma's political leadership and offer opportunities to influence the way in which they look at the world. Pressing for greater openness and exposure to new ideas and new thinking, particularly among members of the up-and-coming generation of leaders is likely, in the long run, to be the most effective means of encouraging change in Burma.

Thank you for extending this opportunity to me to testify today on this pressing and vitally important issue. I welcome any questions you may have.

In: Bangladesh and Burma: Background and Issues ISBN: 978-1-61761-219-0
Editor: Brandon E. Stromberg   © 2011 Nova Science Publishers, Inc.

Chapter 8

TESTIMONY OF DR. THANT MYINT-U, BEFORE THE EAST ASIA SUB-COMMITTEE OF THE SENATE FOREIGN RELATIONS COMMITTEE

The policies of the United States and other Western governments over the past twenty years towards Burma have failed. They have not been helpful in moving the country towards meaningful democratic change and at the same time have largely neglected the country's multiple ethnic and armed conflicts as well as its pressing humanitarian challenges.

As we move towards a very welcome review and adjustment of American policy, I think it's important to reflect on the history behind today's challenges, appreciate the critical and complex watershed Burma now faces, and try to identify pragmatic ways forward.

WAR AND STATE-BUILDING

There is a myth that Burma emerged from British rule in 1948 as a peaceful democracy with all the attributes necessary for later success, only to fall mysteriously into dictatorship and extreme poverty. Burma in 1948 was actually already at civil war, its economy in ruins. And this civil war has continued until today. It is the longest running set of armed conflicts anywhere in the world, setting the Burmese army against an amazing array of battlefield opponents – from the Mujahedeen along the former East Pakistan/Bangladesh border, to remnants of Chiang Kai-Shek's Nationalist Army, to drug-lords, to Beijing-backed communist rebels, to Christian-led ethnic Karen insurgents in the jungles near Thailand.

The Burmese army has been in the field uninterrupted for more than six decades. For the army, the history of these six decades has been the history of their fighting back, to hold the country together, from a time when they barely controlled the then capital Rangoon, to today, when they believe they are within reach of a final victory.

State-building in Burma has gone hand-in-hand with war-making. And the military regime remains at its core a counter-insurgency operation. It was designed and built-up to identify enemies, contain them, and crush them when possible. The men in charge may be motivated by desires for personal power and profit, but they also believe themselves to be patriots. And after two generations of fighting foreign- backed rebellions, they are primed to see foreign conspiracies behind all opposition.

In 1962, the army overthrew the last elected government, in part to pursue its counter-insurgency operations unhindered by civilian oversight. It established what it called The Burmese Way to Socialism, which nationalized all major businesses, expelled the country's Indian merchant class, and sought to isolate Burma from the world, banning nearly all international aid, trade and investment. The military state grew up and consolidated its rule in this self-created isolation. It is its default condition.

These twin legacies – ethnic conflict and international isolation - have been instrumental for the consolidation and continuation of military rule. Progress towards peace, inter-ethnic reconciliation, and the reintegration of Burma into the global community are essential if we are going to see any sustainable transition to civilian government. Yet not only has there been little focus on these issues, but key opportunities in recent years have been missed.

THE END OF BURMESE SOCIALISM AND MISSED OPPORTUNITIES

The early and mid-1990s provided a unique chance to move Burma in the right direction. General Ne Win, dictator of Burma since 1962 was old and ailing and a new generation of generals had come to the fore. The Chinese backed communist insurgency had collapsed and cease-fires were agreed between the Burmese army and more than two dozen different insurgent forces.

While rejecting democratic reform, many in the new leadership wanted to end decades of self-imposed isolation and move towards a more free-market economy. Trade and investment laws were liberalized and tourism encouraged for the first time in decades. Satellite television soon brought the world into millions of Burmese households and travel in and out of the country, both legally and illegally became routine. The government sought development assistance from the UN and the International Financial Institutions. US and international policy should have been to lock in these tentative steps, especially the ceasefires and market reforms, rather than ignore them, impose economic sanctions, cut off assistance, and insist on an immediate democratic transition.

US policy's near singular focus since 1988 on support for the democracy movement led by Daw Aung San Suu Kyi is understandable, especially given ongoing repression and her party's decisive win in the 1990 elections. In the early 1990s I was a staunch supporter of the toughest approach possible towards the regime and argued for comprehensive sanctions. I believe I was wrong and I had changed mind by 1993 when I saw that sanctions were unlikely to ever really pressure the regime and were instead impeding the positive momentum that was there.

There was political repression in Burma, but that's been the constant since 1962. What was different in the 1990s was the end of fighting across the north and northeast and the opening up of the economy. I am convinced that had we embraced these changes and used them as opportunities to move towards a just peace while also reconnecting Burma with the world, the democracy movement would be in a far stronger position today.

THE PROBLEM WITH SANCTIONS

Sanctions have not only been ineffective in promoting democratic reform, they have also been hugely counter-productive in reducing Western influence, reinforcing isolationist tendencies, constraining moves towards market-reforms, and decimating the position of the Burmese professional, managerial and entrepreneurial classes. The last generation of US and UK educated technocrats has now retired or is close to retirement, and very few in the bureaucracy or universities today have had any foreign training. The country is far less prepared for a sustainable democratic transition today than it was in the early 1990s.

We have to remember this: politics in Burma like everything else operates on a landscape cultivated by over sixty years of war and nearly fifty years of military dictatorship. Little will change without first transforming that landscape. Focusing on regime-change at the top will simply not work. Sanctions and related divestment campaigns and campaigns to minimize tourism have drastically reduced chances for the emergence of new and outward looking economic forces. The political economy which has emerged under sanctions, based now on a few extractive industries and trade ties with a handful of regional countries, has proven particularly easy for the incumbent regime to control. Aid restrictions, restrictions on high-level contacts and travel by senior Burmese officials, and embargos on trade and investment all have had the direct if unintended consequence of reinforcing the status quo. And to say that the government's own policies are also to blame do not absolve the role that US and other Western sanctions have played in entrenching poverty and engendering a political economy that is the antithesis of one that could have thrown up positive social change.

We need also to differentiate between punishment and pressure for change. Sanctions may be seen as a form of punishment, in the sense that the regime doesn't like them. But sanctions do not constitute pressure for change, quite the opposite, they strengthen the hand of those who are uninterested in further engagement with the outside world and in particular the West. Real pressure comes with increasing the regime's international exposure, creating new desires, and placing tough options on the table. Having to choose between Western sanctions and a handover of power is simple. But with greater international exposure, a choice between real policy change and improved governance on the one hand or a future as an impoverished dependency of China on the other won't be as easy.

THE PRESENT WATERSHED

Burma now faces an historic watershed, and whatever happens, I am certain that the next 12-18 months will be the most important time in Burmese politics since the failed 1988 uprising.

The current watershed has at least three principal components:

(1) First is the civil war. Burma's civil war may either be nearing an end or entering a new and violent chapter. There still exist more than two dozen distinct ethnic-based insurgent forces, fielding well over 40,000 troops in total. Vast areas of the country, in particular in the north and east are ruled by a mix of Burmese army battalions, insurgent armies and local militia. Though the cease-fire arrangements between the Burmese army and nearly all insurgent forces remain, many are increasingly tenuous. In recent weeks we have seen the oldest of the cease-fires, the twenty-year agreement between the Burmese army and the Kokang militia break down. The coming months may well see successful efforts by the Burmese army to pressure or persuade the various armed groups to transform themselves into quasi-autonomous militia and accept the new constitutional order. But a return to full-scale hostilities, though unlikely, is also far from impossible.

(2) Second is the generational transition within the armed forces. Most if not all the present army leadership will retire in the coming months to be replaced by officers in their late 40s and early 50s. This new generation will be the first to have risen to senior command on the basis of their administrative rather than any significant combat experience, the first without training in the United States, and the first for whom the West, rather than China, has been portrayed as the main strategic threat.

(3) Third is the political transition under the new constitution. Entirely new political structures, including fourteen state and regional governments will be established in 2010 under the new constitution. Central power will at least nominally be bifurcated between a new and powerful president and a new armed forces commander-in-chief. General elections may or may not create an opening for more independent political voices, but the transition to the new constitutional set-up will present at the very least a massive shake-up of existing systems of authority and patronage. We do not know if the leadership will be able to manage the transition as they wish. 2010 may well throw up unexpected new dynamics, especially as they come at the same as major changes in the army's top ranks.

Burma's relationships with her neighbors, in particular China, are also changing fast. The migration of hundreds of thousands if not millions of ethnic Chinese into the country, the rapid expansion of Chinese business interests, and the construction of huge new infrastructure projects linking Burma to southwest China, including a massive Chinese oil pipeline, designed to transport Middle Eastern and African oil across Burma to China's Yunnan province, will have an enormous impact on the Burmese economy and society, especially as there take place during a period of Western economic withdrawal. Burma is already a major exporter of energy to Thailand in the form of natural gas. Burma may soon also export large quantities of natural gas to China and hydroelectric power to China, India and Thailand. How well and how transparently revenues from energy exports are managed will be a key test of any future government.

On China, we have to remember that the present army leadership grew up fighting the Communist Party of Burma, a well-armed Chinese-supported insurgent force that once threatened huge parts of the eastern uplands. There is no love lost between Beijing and Naypyitaw. The present leadership rose up the ranks seeing China as their number one strategic threat and the US as their ally. Many see their present dependence on China as an anomaly, a tactical move that needs correction.

I have visited Burma often in recent years, at least ten times since the beginning of 2007. I've travelled extensively around the country, without escort and few restrictions, and have met hundreds of people, from senior army officers to dissidents to businessmen to local aid workers, including friends and family, some well-off, others struggling each day to feed their families. This is a country where political opposition is violently repressed and there is a obvious desire for greater freedom and government accountability. But it's a also a country where there exists an increasingly vibrant civil society, a heavily- censored but largely privately-owned media, with dozens of newspapers and magazines, widespread access to satellite television and foreign movies, an energetic contemporary music scene, extensive religious freedom, and a weak but resilient private sector. There are literally hundreds of genuinely independent local non-governmental organizations in Burma today, and thousands of community-based organizations, all working to improve living conditions for ordinary people, a young country of 55 million, one of the most ethnically diverse in the world. I say all this not to deemphasize the political repression that exists. Make no mistake – there is little or no political freedom in Burma and the continued detention of an estimated 2,000 prisoners of conscience is rightly seen as unacceptable. But outrage alone changes little. And to move to towards a more results-oriented approach we need to see Burma in all its complexity.

I said that Burma is at a watershed. The ceasefires could collapse leading to a new round of inter-ethnic conflict, a new generation of generals could emerge hostile to the world as well as their own people, and plight of ordinary people could worsen still, even while the rest of Asia moves forward. The demise of current leaders could lead to elite fracture and even state collapse. Alternatively, if more pragmatic views prevail, a freer and more prosperous future may not be so far away. The difference will be determined inside the country, but I believe that are key areas where help from the outside will be significant, as outlined below.

THE IMPORTANCE OF INCREASING HUMANITARIAN ASSISTANCE

The Administration's support for increased humanitarian assistance is extremely welcome and scaling up aid should be a top priority. Burma has the 13th lowest per capita GDP in the world and its child mortality rate is the second-highest rate outside Africa, after Afghanistan. The average family spends an estimated 75% of its small income on food. Burma has the highest HIV rate in Southeast Asia, and malaria, a treatable and preventable disease, is the leading cause of mortality and morbidity.

Yet assistance to the Burmese people in 2007 was less than USD 4 per capita. Though this has increased in response to last year's Cyclone Nargis, aid remains the lowest per capita among the fifty-five poorest countries in the world. By comparison, Zimbabwe receives USD 41 per captia and Sudan USD 55. Tens of thousands of people a year die from treatable diseases. The United Nations, international and national non-governmental organizations are all able to deliver aid directly to needy people. But funding has fallen far short of what is necessary.

Cyclone Nargis opened up the Irrawaddy delta to unprecedented and almost unlimited access by international organizations and international and national non-governmental organizations. Almost four thousand aid workers operate there today in over two thousand villages. In addition to providing life-saving assistance and helping villagers restart their lives and livelihoods, their work is significantly strengthening local civil society. Yet funding for recovery efforts has been only a fraction of what is needed. A unique opportunity to help the Burmese people directly and support local civil society may be squandered without more financial support.

In providing humanitarian assistance, I believe very strongly that we must put all other agendas aside and simply provide aid as best we can to those who require help most and continuously press for access to all needy communities. I believe the US should not only significantly increase humanitarian assistance but actively encourage other donor governments to do the same.

ENABLING CHANGE

Though positive change in all areas will have to come from within, the outside world can make a difference in enabling that change and making it sustainable. I would suggest:

(1) Maximize elite exposure. Every scenario for political change in Burma depends on at least a degree of support from within the military establishment. Yet virtually nothing has been done to try to influence the mind-set of the up and coming officer corps or show them that other paths to stability and development exist. The isolation of the country's leadership from the rest of the world is a key pillar of the status quo, its removal is critical for any lasting political change. Dialogue and cooperation on issues of mutual concern – such as disaster risk reduction - should be used towards this end.

(2) Engage in dialogue on economic reform. Supporters of sanctions are correct when they say that poverty in Burma is not due primarily to sanctions but to the chronic mismanagement of the economy. I favor lifting all economic sanctions, but I also favor more robust efforts to press for economic and related governance reform, separate from any political agenda. This should start with a removal of all restrictions on the United Nations system and the International Financial Institutions, especially the World Bank in engaging the government, including at the highest levels. Efforts to build up the administrative capacity necessary to turn the economy around should be supported, not hindered. As new ministers take up their positions in 2010, they must at least understand the need for more broad-based development, the impact of their own policies, and the options for poverty reduction going forward.

(3) Don't forget the private sector. Humanitarian assistance and other aid is needed now, but Burma, a country rich in natural resources and situated between Asia's emerging economic giants, should make sure it avoids becoming an aid-dependent country. Scaling up international

assistance makes no sense if at the same time we are holding back through broad economic sanctions the possibilities for private sector growth. We need to shift the debate away from sanctions and towards a practical discussion of the kind of trade and investment that would most benefit ordinary people. US sanctions crippled the emerging textile industry and threw 70,000 or more people out of work. Removing the ban on the import of garments from Burma would be a step in the right direction. And if there are specific government obstacles that stand in the way or direct economic engagement with the Burmese private sector (beyond a few top cronies), than the removal of these obstacles should be at the center of dialogue with the authorities.

(4) Build capacity. No sustainable shift from a military to civilian rule will be possible without radically increasing civilian administrative capacity and capacity in society more generally. We cannot underestimate the impact that decades of self-imposed isolation and external sanctions have had on education standards and technocratic skills. Efforts to build capacity – through training and scholarships – should be actively promoted, including through international organizations.

A Democratic Burma

Nothing I have said should suggest any changes in the long term aims we all share – a peaceful, prosperous and democratic Burma. In a country as ethnically and culturally diverse as Burma, only a genuinely liberal democracy with strong local government institutions can, I believe, guarantee lasting stability. A free and economically vibrant Burma at Asia's crossroads is a worthy goal. But we should not underestimate the real and practical challenges that exist between those aims and the situation today. There can be no grand strategy from the outside, only efforts to use and build on opportunities as they come along. And seeing those opportunities depends on being more present on the ground, in direct contact with the Burmese people. This is what a new engagement-oriented approach should be all about.

Thank you.

In: Bangladesh and Burma: Background and Issues   ISBN: 978-1-61761-219-0
Editor: Brandon E. Stromberg   © 2011 Nova Science Publishers, Inc.

Chapter 9

TESTIMONY OF DAVID I. STEINBERG, PROFESSOR, SCHOOL OF FOREIGN SERVICE, GEORGETOWN UNIVERSITY, BEFORE THE U.S. SENATE SUBCOMMITTEE ON ASIA AND PACIFIC AFFAIRS, HEARINGS ON BURMA

Mr. Chairman and Members of the Subcommittee:

It is an honor to have been asked to participate in what I feel has been a long overdue dialogue on Burma/Myanmar[1] problems. I believe there are no easy answers to improving relations and making progress toward our several goals in that country, but I am, and continuously have been, a firm believer in dialogue on this issue within the United States, between the U.S. and other states, as well as with the Burmese themselves, both the government and the opposition. I thus applaud the Obama administration's decision to engage Burma/Myanmar.

I am supportive of this new look, including Senator Webb' s trip to Burma/Myanmar. I believe this also reflects the views of a growing number of Burmese country specialists. It is, as I have written, only a first step. Secretary of State Clinton's statement that sanctions and engagement have both been tried and neither has worked is accurate, but for different actors. The U.S. continuously tried sanctions, gradually strengthening them in response to deteriorating conditions within that country. ASEAN's position has also evolved; it first tried "constructive engagement" that seemed mere economic exploitation. But "worked"for the U.S. meant regime change, and for ASEAN it later meant regime modification. This strategic divergence has perhaps both hindered achieving the changes in that country we seek and made more difficult an effective relationship with ASEAN. Of course, trying to force a government to leave power in the hope that one would then engage them is a non-sequitur. The new position, articulated by the Secretary of State, that sanctions and dialogue are not necessarily contradictory is accurate as far as it goes; it is a relatively temporary state, however, that should be resolved over some reasonable period, but it does not preclude other actions that might mitigate tensions and differences.

I believe most foreign observers want to see Burma/Myanmar make democratic progress and improve the well being of the diverse Burmese peoples. We are aware of and deplore the misguided economic, social, and ethnic policies that for a half-century have made what was predicted to be the richest nation in the region into the poorest. We share goals on its political and economic future, but have differences in the tactics needed to secure these objectives. But by isolating Burma/Myanmar, we have in effect played into the hands of Burmese military leaders who thus justify their position that a garrison state under their control is necessary because of perceived foreign threats and the potential break up of the Union.

The U.S. in the past has not tried engagement and dialogue, although the U.S. now want them and the National League for Democracy (NLD) has called for them for some time. We now believe that the military must be part of any political solution; this is a new, evolved, and more positive position, and one now shared by the NLD and Aung San Suu Kyi. Our consideration of Burma/Myanmar has concentrated on governance issues to the virtual exclusion of a broad range of problems that should be analyzed. Indeed, by concentrating essentially on politics we may have missed opportunities to affect positively other deplorable conditions in that country.

We understand and sympathize with those who have suffered egregious human rights abuses. We understand the plight and frustration of those exiles who want a better Burma, and who place political change as the primary factor in this process. This approach, however, has not worked, and, in contrast, I would suggest we start by focusing on the Burmese people—their sorry condition and how to alleviate their plight. There is a major socioeconomic crisis in that state, one that was early recognized by the UN but exacerbated by the Nargis cyclone, and one that requires pervasive reform and extensive assistance. It is also one that the government denies.

In this hearing, I have been asked to testify on three basic points:

[1] Prospects for political reform and the potential role of the U.S. in promoting democracy and the upcoming elections;
[2] The economic and strategic implications of unilateral U.S. sanctions;
[3] Steps that can and should be taken to improve the U.S.-Burma relationship.

[1] Prospects for political reform and the potential role of the U.S. in promoting democracy and the upcoming elections.

If we are to evaluate the prospects for reform, we must first understand that the present attitudes and positions of the U.S. and Burmese governments are virtually diametrically opposite with starkly divergent appraisals of the past and present reality. Both sets of perceptions reflect differing cultural backgrounds and different priorities, even how power and authority are viewed. Trying to reconcile these irreconcilable perceptions will not be productive now; it is time to concentrate on how to affect the future.

We may distinguish short term potential U.S. responses to encouraging the democratic aspects of the forthcoming 2010 elections from those that could foster democracy in the longer term. These two aspects of reaction are not seamless, but could produce antithetical results if unbalanced. Concentrating on the short term period before the 2010 elections and possible disappointments therein, while ignoring the longer-term future, may obscure more distant democratic opportunities. Considering only the longer term approach could vitiate chances, however tenuous, for early progress. The results of the planned 2010 elections might result in a new political dynamic, one that eventually opens some political space that could evolve into more effective governance. We should not ignore that possibility.

The prospects for political changes before the 2010 elections, however, seem dim. The military will not renegotiate the new constitutional provisions approved in 2008, as the NLD has demanded. Whether the NLD would participate in the elections if allowed, is still uncertain. Various parties, both those government backed and opposition, are in the process of formation in advance of articulated state regulations. These elections from the junta's viewpoint are in part designed to wipe out the 1990 election results which the NLD swept, so the NLD has a dilemma: to participate destroys their previous claim to authority, but to abstain marginalizes them even further. The political end game is fast approaching, and the NLD needs to salvage its position or it may disintegrate or split. Whatever happens to the NLD, other opposition parties will participate and have some voice (rather *sotto voce*) in the new government, but one in which the military will have veto power on critical issues. There is no question but that the government and the legislature emerging from the 2010 elections will be dominated by the military, which will have 25 percent of the seats reserved for active- duty officers and thus can prevent unwanted amendments to the constitution, which require 75 percent approval. Military control will be taut on issues it regards as vital to the country and over its own defense affairs, but may allow some avenues for debate and compromise.

The U.S. should recognize that these elections will take place, and that their results, however fair or unfair, will strongly influence the future of Burma/Myanmar over the next half-decade and longer. We must deal with that reality. We should continue to call for the release of all political prisoners, the early promulgation of a liberal political party registration law and voting legislation, the ability of all parties to campaign openly and relaxation of the press censorship law so that parties may distribute campaign literature. We should encourage the UN and ASEAN to request permission to monitor the elections and vote counting. Although unlikely to be approved, the effort should be made. The U.S. might consider, through ASEAN or the UN, to supplying technical assistance and computer software for accurate ballot counting. This has been done in some other countries. These important considerations, however, even if ignored and even if the military were to engage in acts against the minorities or opposition that are reprehensible, should not terminate dialogue and a staged process of attempting to improve relations to mitigate these vital poroblems. I believe the Burmese administration sadly had no intention of allowing Aung San Suu Kyi out of house arrest before the elections, and that her trial was unnecessary for that purpose, for the junta would have found some rationale for her detention in any case.

A longer term approach to encouraging democracy in Burma/Myanmar should also be instituted at the same time. Yet the role of the U.S. in affecting positive change is limited by Burmese perceptions of the U.S., the U.S. internal political process, and U.S. past actions related to Burma/Myanmar.

The junta is suspicious of the U.S. There are two decades of distrust that strongly influence present and future relations. This heritage may not be insurmountable, but it is significant. The Burmese fear a U.S. invasion, however illogical that may seem to Americans. This accounts for their refusal to allow the U.S. to deliver directly relief supplies to the Burmese in Cyclone Nargis. Our cry for regime change and the "outpost of tyranny" characterization are not forgotten. Our support for dissident groups along the

Thai border reinforces these fears, as does the potential role of Thailand as a perceived surrogate and ally of U.S. policy in the region. The U.S. has held the Burmese to a different, and more stringent, standard that we have for other authoritarian regimes with which we deal in terms of the political parties, religious freedom, and even human rights. In the region, China, Vietnam, and Laos immediately come to mind. Strong congressional and public antipathy to dialogue, let alone more productive relationships with the regime, often center on the role and fate of Nobel Laureate Aung San Suu Kyi, and affect U.S. policy changes. Recent indications that she is willing to reconsider sanctions that she has in the past encouraged are welcome.

Several approaches to longer-range problems should be considered. The build up of indigenous civil society through the international NGO community is one element in the attempt to encourage more pluralism over the longer term and to begin to alleviate suffering and problems through local organizations more cognizant of local needs. Even under authoritarian regimes, civil society has important functions, and ironically the government since 1988 has allowed more civil society groups, both foreign and indigenous, to function then under the 1962 military government, although it has done so with political restrictions.

More basic human needs assistance (humanitarian aid) is necessary (health, education, nutrition, agriculture) to help the society out of the economic mire in which perhaps half the population is either under or at the World Bank defined poverty line. The education system may have been expanded, as the government claims, but the quality has been destroyed. Health care is dismal–said to be the world's second worst. Thirty percent of children are malnourished to some degree. The per capita foreign assistance in Burma/Myanmar is about twenty times less than that provided to Laos. In a country like Burma/Myanmar, where the state intervenes administratively and personally at virtually all levels, it may be necessary to work with state institutions (such as the health system) if the people are to be helped. Depending on how this is done, it may be a small price to pay to assist the population.

In essence, by improving education and health, the groundwork of a more competent and vital populace will be developed that would better contribute to any new, and eventually more representative, government. Without such improvements, when changes come, as they inevitably will, a new more open government will be saddled with even more difficult problems that might have been earlier mitigated.

Third, there is one thing the U.S. does well–that is train people. Building up human capital is a primary requirement if the state is to progress. Modern training in basic human needs fields and in economics and related disciplines is essential. The country has lost perhaps three percent of its total population through migration due to political and economic problems and lack of opportunity, as well as through warfare and the threat of violence. Although two percent may be workers and undereducated minorities, one percent is an educated group who might have been the backbone of any new liberal administration. Even should internal conditions improve, many, perhaps most, would not return because they have become rooted in other societies. Either directly or through ASEAN, modern training should be provided either in the U.S. or in the region. This is essential for future progress. The international NGOs employ some 10,000 Burmese and the UN some 3,000 more. They and others should be given the opportunity to acquire advanced skills so they can contribute to future development under improved governance.

The U.S. should recognize that the military is and will be for a long period a cardinal socio-economic force. The military now controls all avenues of social mobility in that society. This was not true in the civilian period. Beyond the public sector, they also have important economic assets in terms of military owned and run conglomerates that influence and even control large elements of economic activity. Those families that are ambitious and may even be opposed to the military in their administrative roles now send their sons into the military as the only real avenue of mobility and advancement. Alternative avenues, such as the private sector and other autonomous institutions, must be developed if there is to be an eventual balance between civilian and military authority. Real change will only come when these new avenues of social mobility are opened. This will take a long time, as it took in South Korea, and as it is now taking in Thailand and in Indonesia. The military will remain a vital element in that society for the foreseeable future. This should be recognized and efforts made both to help provide alternative avenues of mobility and also to broaden military attitudes and knowledge in terms of national development needs and social change. Militaryto-military contacts are important, and I think it was wise of the U.S. to continue to have a military attaché attached to the embassy in Rangoon, in contrast to the EU, which withdrew them in 1996 and assigned them all to Bangkok.

[2] The economic and strategic implications of unilateral U.S. sanctions

[2a] Economic implications of sanctions

Although some in the Congress wanted to impose Cuba-like sanctions in 1997, cooler heads prevailed. The four tranches of sanctions (1988, 1997, 2003, 2008) have had several effects. It has denied market access to the U.S. It has resulted in other states, especially China, increasing its market share. It has also resulted in a loss of jobs for the Burmese peoples, a country already wracked with high un- and under-employment. And it has not resulted in an improvement in human rights or working conditions for the Burmese. In addition, it has lost to U.S. businesses markets and some jobs that would have been important, but it has not injured the Burmese government, which has simply substituted materials and services from other states, including some from our allies. Sanctions have been, admittedly, the moral high ground, but they have accomplished none of the U.S. objectives of reform and change. The present U.S. sanctions policy toward Burma/Myanmar illustrates how easy it is to impose sanctions, and how difficult it is to eliminate them once imposed. Yet, while encouraging the private sector, we should remember that although it is an important avenue for development, it is not a panacea. Those who consider that fostering foreign investment and encouraging the indigenous private sector will early bring democracy had better be prepared for an extended wait–witness South Korea (1961-1987) and Taiwan (1949-1992).

[2b] Strategic Issues

Sanctions and an absence of dialogue have resulted in a lack of public recognition, until recently, of the strategic importance of Burma/Myanmar in the region. The need in a democracy to discuss publicly the multiple bases of foreign policy has been ignored–we have concentrated on human rights and democracy alone. These are important, necessary elements of foreign policy, but not the complete picture. If the American public and the Congress are to support any administration's foreign policy, the full range of U.S. interests needs articulation.

Burma/Myanmar is the nexus on the Bay of Bengal. It will be a major issue in future China-India relations. Both countries are rapidly rising in economic terms and are likely to be eventual rivals. Chinese extensive penetration of Myanmar prompted a complete change in Indian policy from being most vehemently against the junta to a supporter and provider of foreign aid. A secondary motive was to mitigate the rebellions in the Indian Northeast, where rebel organizations have had sanctuaries in Myanmar. India bid for Burmese off-shore natural gas, but China has basically dominated that field and will build two pipelines across Myanmar to Yunnan Province–one for Burmese natural gas and the second for Middle- Eastern crude oil. China is supporting more than two dozen hydroelectric dams in Burma/Myanmar with important potentially negative environmental effects. One strategic Chinese concern is the bottleneck of the Straits of Malacca through which 80 percent of imported Chinese energy transits. Should the straits be blockaded, Chinese defense and industrial capacities could be negatively affected, and drops in employment could threaten political stability. Chinese activities in Myanmar mitigate this concern. In reverse, some Japanese military have said that the ability of the Chinese to import oil through Myanmar and avoid the Malacca Straits and the South China Sea is not in Japan's national interests. India is also concerned with potential Chinese influence in the Bay of Bengal through Burma/Myanmar.

The Burmese have used the issue of China in their analysis of U.S. attitudes toward that regime. Burmese military intelligence has specifically written that the interest of the U.S. in regime change in Myanmar was because Myanmar was the weakest link in the U.S.' containment policy toward China. Although the original statement was published in 1997, it had been reprinted 28 times by 2004. The Burmese have not understood that the U.S. concern was focused on human rights, but perhaps their statements were designed to, and have reinforced, the importance to the Chinese of support to the Burmese regime and thus increased Chinese assistance both economically and militarily. It should be understood, however, that Burma/Myanmar is not a client state of China. The Burmese administration is fearful of the roles and inordinate influences of all foreign governments, including the Chinese, the Indian, and the U.S., and with considerable historical justification. The Chinese government for years supported the insurrection of the Burma Communist Party, India is said to have assisted Kachin and Karen rebels and in the colonial period controlled much of the economy, and the Thai a multitude of insurgent groups. The U.S. previously supported the Chinese Nationalist (Kuomintang) remnant forces in Burma. More sustained dialogue could help us understand the strategic dynamics of Burma/Myanmar, including its obscured relationship with North Korea.

Although the U.S. under three presidents (Clinton, Bush, and Obama) have invoked the phrase "The actions and policies of the Government of the Union of Burma continue to pose an unusual and extraordinary threat to the national security and foreign policy of the United States," this statement is simply an administrative mantra and gross exaggeration because this language must be used (under the Emergency Economic Powers Act of 1997) if the executive branch wishes to impose unilateral sanctions (it was used recently in the case of North Korea). That does not mean there are no problems. Non-traditional security issues abound, such illegal migration, trafficking, narcotics (now, metamphetamines), health issues, but none of them reach the status of an "extraordinary threat" either within the region or to the United States. Although Burma/Myanmar was once rightly castigated for its heroin production (although the U.S. has never accused the government itself as receiving funds from the trade-- it tolerated money laundering activities), the U.S. *National Drug Threat Assessment of 2009* indicates that opium production dropped significantly since 2002, and that since 2006 the U.S. could not chemically identify any heroin imported into the U.S. from Burma/Myanmar. Rather than assisting in the improvement of health as a cross-national problem, the U.S. refused to support the Global Fund, which was to provide $90 million in that country over five years to counter HIV/AIDS, tuberculosis, and malaria. The Europeans instead funded the Three Disease fund with $100 million of the same period to fight the same diseases.

We should be concerned about the stability of the state and administration. China, India, ASEAN, the U.S. and other countries want stability. Although the Burmese state appears strong in terms of its coercive control, poor and deteriorating economic conditions, internal displacement of peoples, delicate and potentially fluid and explosive minority relations, arbitrary and repressive military actions, political frustration, and the influx of massive illegal Chinese immigrants (estimated at perhaps two million) and their increasing hold over the economy are elements that could easily result in internal violence, ethnic rioting (as in 1967), and deteriorating conditions that are against the interests of all external actors and the Burmese people themselves. We should be trying to convince the Burmese administration itself that it is the interests of their country to reform, for only then will stability be possible.

[3] Steps that can and should be taken to improve the U.S.-Burma relationship.

The Burmese authorities have been told by many that improvement in U.S.-Burmese relations will require significant actions by the Burmese themselves to justify changes in U.S. policy. Political attitudes in the U.S. preclude immediate or early lessening of the sanctions regimen without such reciprocal actions. In the first instance, however, increases in humanitarian assistance (basic human needs, such as health, education, nutrition, agriculture) are essential.

Step-by-step negotiations are a reasonable way to proceed, perhaps the only way. Signals have been sent by both sides that some changes are desirable, but good words alone will not work. And whatever the U.S. proposes must be done with the support of both the executive and legislative branches, in contrast to an abortive executive attempt to improve relations on narcotics in 2002 that faltered in the Congress. It should be understood that such staged dialogue by both sides is not appeasement, and that both sanctions and engagement are tactics to secure objectives, not ends in themselves.

It should also be understood that as a general commentary on such negotiations, expecting the Burmese to humiliate themselves before any foreign power and give in to foreign demands, whether from the Chinese or the U.S., is a recipe for a failed negotiations. Public posturing should be avoided, and quiet diplomacy take place to which the Burmese can respond to the need for progress and change within their own cultural milieu and with a means of explaining to their own people that these are indigenous solutions to indigenous problems. Unconditional surrender, which the U.S. has advocated on many occasions, is not a negotiating or dialogue position.

To start the process, the U.S. should approve of a new Burmese ambassador (previously nominated) to Washington. The last one left in November 2004 after the ouster of Prime Minister Khin Nyunt in Burma/Myanmar and had nothing to do with sanctions issues. The administration should also be prepared to nominate an ambassador to Myanmar, even though there may be strong and negative congressional reactions. That person would be different from the ambassadorial position as coordinator under the Lantos 2008 sanctions legislation, and the choice of that person is important if there is to be credible dialogue with the government, since it calls for direct talks with the Burmese.

There are also areas where our interests overlap, and where coordinated efforts could be productive in themselves and in trying to build the confidence required if relations in other fields are to improve. We have a mutual interest in the environment, and indeed the U.S. has been working with the Burmese on protection of wildlife. There is much we could accomplish together and an urgent need. There are cooperative relations that could prove important in disaster preparation, for Burma/Myanmar is subject to earthquakes and cyclones that annually devastate the Burmese coast, although not normally with the force of Nargis. There is still work to be done on the missing-in-action U.S. soldiers whose planes went down in Burma flying from India to China during World War II. There are the needs of the minorities who have been generally excluded from development. An especial reference should be made to the Rohingyas, the Muslim minority on the Bangladesh border who have remained stateless and who have suffered the most. Although the U.S. has concentrated its attention on political issues and human rights in general, the minority question in Burma/Myanmar is the most important, long-range and complex issue in that multi-cultural state. There is a need to find some "fair" manner in the Burmese context for their development, the protection of their cultural identity, and the sharing of the assets of the state. Within the unity of Burma/Myanmar, the U.S. might be able to contribute to this process. Further, improving relations with Burma/Myanmar will help strengthen our relations with ASEAN. The U.S. has made significant and welcome progress in the recent past, and the dialogue with Burma/Myanmar would help that process. The U.S. signing the ASEAN Treaty of Amity and Cooperation in July 2009 was a forward step.

In a variety of authoritarian states, the U.S. has supported programs that were designed to improve justice and the rule of law. Although this may seem counterintuitive, such programs could be of value in training individuals and assisting institutions to administer justice more fairly when they are in a position to do so. Although the United States objected when Australia started some human rights training in Burma/Myanmar (as it had done in Indonesia under Suharto), the exposure of key individuals with some responsibilities for dealing with such problems would be an investment for a time when they are able to use that knowledge to further goals we all share. The U.S. could join with the Australian program for ASEAN designed to provide counter-terrorism training courses at the Jakarta Centre for Law Enforcement. Burma/Myanmar has cooperated with the U.S. on some counter-terrorism activities, including but not limited to authorizing overflights of the country after 9/11.

The U.S. use of the term for the name of the state, Burma, rather than the military designated term, Myanmar (an old term, but one used in the modern written language) is simply a result of following the NLD. The military regard that as an insult. Although I believe the change in name was a tactical error, especially during a year when the government was trying to encourage tourism, many states, even those of which we disapproved, have changed their names and place names and the U.S. has followed. It did, however, take a couple of decades for the U.S. to change Peking to Beijing.

The Burmese need to respond to any U.S. overture. One might suggest to the junta that in light of the good performance of the international NGOs during the Nargis crisis, that the January 2006 stringent and deleterious regulations on their operation be waived, and that new ones formulated in collaboration with the NGO community. We want greater changes, but this start would be significant and allow the international NGOs to make a greater contribution to development in that country. Increases in humanitarian assistance, required in any event, would be greatly facilitated by such action.

If the Burmese were to respond to this step-by-step process, and if the 2010 elections were carried out in some manner with widespread campaigning and participation regarded as in a responsible manner (admittedly a term with strong cultural roots), then the U.S. could withdraw is opposition to multilateral assistance from the World Bank or Asian Development Bank if that government were to adhere to the bank's new requirements for transparency and good governance. Burmese economic policy formulation is opaque, and such activities might not only provided needed light, but also encourage a sense of reality among the military leadership, some of whom are said to be insulated from the dire conditions in the country. The U.S. could modify its sanctions approach; some have called for more targeted sanctions that could be an indicator of gradual improvement of relations. If we want to influence the new generation in Burma/Myanmar, why do we then under the sanctions program prohibit the children and grandchildren of the military leadership from studying in the U.S.? These are just some of the people from influential families whose attitudes toward the U.S. we should hope to change. If the sanctions policy were to be modified and gradually rescinded, it would require significant reforms for that to happen.

It is probable that not much will be possible before the 2010 Burmese elections, that date of which has not yet been announced. Until then, it is likely the Burmese government will be primarily focused on actions leading up to that activity and have limited interest in important changes. That does not mean we should not try to affect change in that period.

Some general comments may be in order. It is important in any international negotiations that the U.S. not be wedded to the interests of any particular foreign leader or group, for although their objectives may be similar, their tactics, views, and immediate interests may differ from U.S. national interests. U.S. policy should not be held hostage to foreign attitudes, however benign.

In negotiations, it is also important not to characterize the military as we have in the past with "rogue, " "pariah," "thuggish," and other such terms. The regime has to be treated with civility or any discussions will fail. We conceive grammatically and politically of the military as singular, but in fact it is plural, and there are elements who are not corrupt, who have a sense of idealism in their own terms, who want to do something for their own society, and who recognize that improved governance internally and better relations externally are part of that process. We should understand the potential diversity of the military and seek to identify and encourage positive thinking on their part.

The question will be asked whether dialogue and negotiations as suggested in the paper will provide an added degree of legitimacy to the present military regime or one evolving from the 2010 elections of which the U.S. may not approve. Any relationship involves a delicate equation in which one attempts to gauge the benefits and the disadvantages involved toward reaching the goals that have been set. In the case of Burma/Myanmar, I believe the advantages to the United States and to the peoples of Burma/Myanmar outweigh any slight fillip of legitimization the regime may claim. I believe the people of that country are more astute.

We should also negotiate with the Burmese on the basis that their primary national goal of the unity of the Union is a shared goal of the U.S., and that we do not want to see the balkanization of Burma, but that the actions of their own government and the attitudes of some of the military convey the impression that they are an occupying army in some minority areas, and this undercuts the willingness of some of the minorities to continue under Burman rule, and thus the ability of that government to reach its goal. It is in the interests of the region and the world not to see a break up of the country, but that unity can only be achieved through internal respect and dignity among all the peoples of the state, and through real developmental efforts to which the U.S. could contribute under conditions to be negotiated.

I am not sanguine about early progress, but what has been done in the past months and this hearing itself are important beginnings and should be continued and expanded.

Thank you for giving me this opportunity to contribute to the process of dialogue.

David I. Steinberg is Distinguished Professor of Asian Studies, School of Foreign Service, Georgetown University. His most recent volume is *Burma/Myanmar: What Everyone Needs to Know* (Oxford University Press).

End Notes

[1] In 1989, the military changed the name of the state from Burma to Myanmar, an old written form. The opposition, followed by the U.S., has never accepted that change as from a government they regard as illegitimate. The UN and other countries use Myanmar; thus, the name of the country has become a surrogate indicator of political inclination. Here, both are

used and without political implications. Burmese is used for the citizens of that country and as an adjective.

In: Bangladesh and Burma: Background and Issues ISBN: 978-1-61761-219-0
Editor: Brandon E. Stromberg   © 2011 Nova Science Publishers, Inc.

Chapter 10

Testimony of David C. Williams, Executive Director, Center for Consitutional Democracy, John S. Hastings Professor of Law, Indiana University Maurer School of Law, before the Senate Foreign Relations Subcommittee on East Asia and Pacific Affairs, Hearing on "U.S. Policy toward Burma: Its Impact and Effectiveness"

Chairman Webb, Senator Inhofe, I thank you for the opportunity to testify during this second anniversary of the Saffron Revolution. Chairman Webb, please let me congratulate you on your trip to Southeast Asia. I am grateful that you want to consider the many ways that the US might promote democracy in Burma, beyond just the issue of sanctions. Finally, and on a more personal note, please let me thank you for trying to secure the release of Le Cong Dinh, who is the secretary general of the Democratic Party of Vietnam. I advise the DPV on constitutional reform. Dinh hosted my family for a two week visit in the spring, and on the day we left, he was arrested and remains in prison. We pray for his well-being and thank you for your efforts.

But we are here to talk about Burma, not Vietnam, which is a very different place. And when thinking about US policy toward Burma, it is important to focus on the realities, even when they are uncomfortable. I would like to highlight two realities that I know from personal experience.

Here is the first reality: the SPDC is committing mass atrocities against the ethnic minorities. I know this because I advise many of the ethnic groups on constitutional reform, and I've spent a lot of time with them, witnessing conditions on the ground.

Here is the second reality: even if the 2010 elections are free and fair, which they won't be, they won't bring about civilian rule because the constitution does not provide for it--a partially civilian government, yes, but civilian rule, no. I teach constitutional law, and I consult in a number of countries, and this is one of the worst constitutions I have ever seen. The SPDC has done a good job of disguising what they've done, but underneath the attractive labeling, there is a blueprint for continued military rule.

Regarding the ethnic minorities, when you leave Rangoon and get up into the hills, things seem very different. I work a lot with the Karen, who are the Scots-Irish of Southeast Asia.[1] They are a hill people, musical, clannish, and tough. They have long been dominated by a distant government, which they have learned to distrust. As a group, they are the gentlest and most loving people I know. But all of them were born fighting, because their government is slaughtering them as we speak. And they need our help.

Burma's problems began in ethnic conflict, and they will continue until the underlying issues are addressed. Some people seem to think that Burma's struggle is between one woman, Aung San Suu Kyi, who wants democracy, and one man, Than Shwe, who doesn't. But even if democracy comes to Burma, the troubles will not end until the needs and demands of the minorities have been answered. The resistance groups are not strong enough to overthrow the regime, but the regime is not strong enough to crush the resistance.

Conditions in central Burma are bad, but in the ethnic areas there is suffering on a biblical scale, in every way comparable to Darfur. The military is making war on a civilian population, and its actions likely constitute crimes against humanity. The United Nations has found that soldiers routinely commit rape with impunity, and rape appears to be a policy for population control.[2] By one UN estimate, officers commit 83% of these rapes, and 61% are gang rapes.[3] When outsiders try to investigate, officers commonly threaten to cut the tongues and slice the throats of any villager who speaks to them.[4]

But these bald statistics cannot tell the human dimension of the suffering; reading the individual accounts is excruciating. As just one example: "Ms.

Naang Khin, aged 22, and her sister, Ms. Naang Lam, aged 19, were reportedly raped by a patrol of SPDC troops . . . when they were reaping rice at their farm . . . Their father was tied to a tree. Afterwards, the two sisters were taken to a forest by the troops. Their dead bodies were found by villagers some days later dumped in a hole."[5]

The Tatmadaw also uses forced labor[6] and is probably the greatest conscriptor of child soldiers in the world.[7] The military does not generally attack the armed resistance forces; instead, it burns or mortars villages, over 3000 villages since 1996.[8] And this has been going on for years, creating one of the worst refugee crises in the world—one million plus between 1996 and 2006 and one half million still displaced today.[9] One woman had to run for days through the jungle immediately after giving birth, carrying her baby in her arms. That baby grew up, got an American law degree, and she is now a research fellow in my Center. And she is a miracle of survival.

China cannot ignore the ethnic minorities, because it has had to deal with a wave of refugees, driven there by the SPDC's attacks. Beijing publicly rebuked the regime for creating regional instability, which of course would be grounds for Security Council intervention. In other words, on this point, China and the US appear to be on the same page with respect to Burma: we all want the attacks to end.

So what policy recommendations follow from this reality?

First, the US should supply humanitarian aid not just through Rangoon but also across the borders to the ethnic minority areas. The programs in central Burma cannot get out into the hills, and as a result, the people who are suffering the most are receiving the least.

Second, the State Department has told us that the regime wants closer relations and will appoint an interlocutor. But if we are going to enter dialogue with the junta, we must first demand an immediate end to the attacks on civilian populations. Otherwise, we will be directly dealing with murderers still in the midst of a killing spree.

Third, Burma will never know peace or justice until there are trilateral talks between the SPDC, the democracy forces, and the ethnic minorities. The international community has long known this truth, but the regime has proved unwilling. If we are going to open dialogue with the regime, we must insist that they engage not just with the NLD but also with the minorities.

My second subject is the 2010 elections. We all would like to hope that they will usher in a new era of possibility. But in fact, they won't bring peace or civilian rule. The runup to the elections has already brought more violence, not less. Overwhelmingly, the resistance armies have rejected the SPDC's demand that they become border guard units after the elections, and the SPDC has responded by attacking the Kokang. The conflict will only increase when the regime moves against larger groups: we will soon see fighting with the United Wa State Army, the Kachin Independence Army, and others. We know for a fact that the Burmese military is gearing up for offensives around the country and that the resistance groups are getting ready to resist attacks. The mountains will run with blood.

So the elections won't bring peace; they also won't bring civilian rule. Some think that we should try to ensure that the elections are free and fair—but that really matters only if the elections will actually lead to civilian rule, which they won't. The constitution allows the Tatmadaw to keep however much control it likes.

I clerked for Ruth Bader Ginsburg years ago, and she always taught us to read laws very closely. This constitution bears particularly close reading, because it is much worse than is generally reported. A lot of people worry that the Tatmadaw will dominate the government because they will appoint 25% of the various legislative bodies. But there's a much bigger problem: under the constitution, the the Tatmadaw is not subject to civilian government, and it writes its own portfolio. It can do whatever it wants.

The Constitution guarantees the power of the Tatmadaw in its section on "Basic Principles"—a clear sign that the framers thought the role of the Defence Services to be fundamental. Article 20(b) provides that the military will run its own show without being answerable to anyone: "The Defence Services has [sic] the right to independently administer and adjudicate all affairs of the armed forces." The constitution defines the "affairs of the armed forces" so broadly as to encompass anything that the Tatmadaw might want to do. Article 6(f) provides that among the "Union's consistent objectives" is "enabling the Defence Services to participate in the National political leadership role of the State." Article 20(e) further assigns the Tatmadaw primary responsibility for "safeguarding the non-disintegration of the Union, the non-disintegration of National solidarity and the perpetuation of sovereignty." This regime has frequently found a threat to "National solidarity" when people merely disagree with it; it is prepared to slaughter peacefully protesting monks. There is no reason to think that after 2010, the Tatmadaw will think differently.

Because the Tatmadaw's responsibilities are so broadly and vaguely defined, the question of who will have the power to interpret their scope is critical. The constitution answers that question clearly: the Tatmadaw will have the power to determine the powers of the Tatmadaw. Article 20(f) assigns the Tatmadaw primary responsibility "for safeguarding the Constitution." But if the military is the principal protector of the constitution, then the military will presumably have the final authority to determine its meaning, so as to know what to protect. And indeed, Article 46 implicitly confirms this conclusion: it gives the Constitutional Tribunal power to declare legislative and executive actions unconstitutional, but it conspicuously omits the power to declare military actions unconstitutional. In other words, the Tatmadaw has the final authority to interpret the scope of its own constitutional responsibilities. Most first year law students have read a famous portion of Bishop Hoadly's Sermon, preached before the King in 1717: "Whoever hath an absolute authority to interpret any written or spoken laws, it is he who is truly the lawgiver, to all intents and purposes, and not the person who first spoke or wrote them."[10] And under the Burmese constitution, the Tatmadaw will be "truly the lawgiver," not the people elected in 2010.

The Constitution further ensures that the Tatmadaw will have the power to control the citizenry on a day-to-day basis. Under Article 232(b)(ii), the Commander-in-Chief will appoint the Ministers for Defence, Home Affairs, and Border Affairs. The military's control over home affairs is especially ominous because it gives the Defence Services broad power over the lives of ordinary citizens in their daily lives.

The military's control over Home Affairs (as well as Defence and Border Affairs) will constitute a military fiefdom, not part of the civilian government in any meaningful sense. The Commander-in-Chief will have power to name the ministers without interference from any civilian official. The President may not reject the Commander-inChief's names; he must submit the list to the legislature. See Article 232(c). The legislature may reject those names only if they do not meet the formal qualifications for being a minister, such as age and residence. See Article 232(d). Theoretically, the legislature could impeach those ministers under Article 233, but the Commander-in-Chief would merely re-appoint a new minister acceptable to him.

In addition, these ministers will continue to serve in the military, so they will be under orders from the Commander-in-Chief, not from the President. See Article 232(j)(ii). In other words, the Commander-in-Chief will be administering home affairs, immune from interference by the civilian government. Theoretically—again—the legislature might try to pass statutes controlling the Tatmadaw, but recall—again--that under Article 20(b), the Tatmadaw has the "right to independently administer and adjudicate all affairs of the armed forces."

The independent power of the Tatmadaw over ordinary citizens includes the power to impose military discipline on the entire population. Article 20 provides: "The Defence Services has the right to administer for participation of the entire people in Union security and defence." In other words, the military may forcibly enlist the whole citizenry into a militia so as to maintain internal "security." And, again, the civilian government has no control over the military's operations. After the elections, Burma will be a military dictatorship just as much as now.

In short, during normal times, the Tatmadaw has constitutional power to do anything it wants without interference from the civilian government. But if it ever tires of the civilian government, it can declare a state of emergency and send everyone else home. On this subject, the constitution uses a bait and switch approach: in one section, it creates a process for declaring a state of emergency in which the civilian government will have a role; but in another section, it specifies that the military may re-take power entirely on its own initiative. Thus, in Chapter XI, the constitution provides for the declaration of a state of emergency in which the military would assume all powers of government, see Article 419, but it would require presidential agreement before the fact, see Article 417, as well as legislative ratification afterwards, see Article 421. But in Chapter I on Basic Principles, Article 40(c) provides for a very different, alternative process in which the Commander-in-Chief can act at his own discretion: "If there arises a state of emergency that could cause disintegration of the Union, disintegration of national solidarity and loss of sovereign power or attempts therefore by wrongful forcible means such as insurgency or violence, *the Commander-in-Chief of the Defence Services has the right to take over and exercise State sovereign power in accord with the provisions of this Constitution.*" (emphasis supplied). To be sure, the Tatmadaw may seize power only if "national solidarity" is threatened, but as already shown, the military has unreviewable authority to decide whether such a threat exists.

In other words, the Tatmadaw can seize control just as it did in 1962, and this time it will be legal. The whole constitution is based on a "wait and see" strategy: if the civilian government does what the Tatmadaw wants, then it will be allowed to rule; if not, then not. This constitution is not a good faith gesture toward democracy; it's a cynical attempt to buy off international pressure.

So what policy recommendations follow from this reality? We should certainly try to ensure that the elections are free and fair, unlike the referendum on the constitution, if the regime will permit us. But our greatest focus should be on constitutional change, so that someday Burma might witness civilian rule. That change should occur before the elections, but if it must wait until after, then we should hold the SPDC to its word: it has always claimed that it could not negotiate with the opposition because it was only a transitional government—for twenty years. After the elections, that excuse will be gone.

If the US opens dialogue with the regime, it must demand that the regime simultaneously open dialogue with its own citizens. But in order to make demands, we must be able to give the regime something. If we relax sanctions now, rather than in response to real progress, then we will have that much less to offer—as Secretary Clinton and the sixty- six co-sponsors of the sanctions have recognized. And let us speak plainly: if we try to compete with China for influence over a military autocracy, we will always be at a disadvantage because there are some things we just won't do. We win only if we can shift the game, only if through multilateral diplomacy we can get the regime to stop killing its people and to allow civilian rule. Making premature concessions won't shift the game; it will only give the game away.

End Notes

[1] For more on the Scots-Irish, see James Webb, Born Fighting: How the Scots-Irish Shaped America (2005).
[2] See *Crimes in Burma: A Report by International Human Rights Clinic at Harvard Law School* at 51-64. This definitive report analyzes and synthesizes the United Nations reports documenting human rights abuses in Burma.
[3] *See id.* at 59.
[4] *See id.* at 60.
[5] *See id.* at 55.
[6] *See id.* at 15-16.
[7] *See* Human Rights Watch, *"My Gun was as Tall as Me ": Child Soldiers in Burma* (2002).
[8] *See Crimes in Burma, supra* note 1, at 40.
[9] *See id.*
[10] See Choper, Fallon, Kamisar, and Shiffrin, Constitutional Law: Cases—Comments—Questions, page 1 (Ninth Edition 2001).

CHAPTER SOURCES

The following chapter have been previously published:

Chapter 1 – This is an edited reformatted and augmented version of a Congressional Research Service publication, report R41194, April 1, 2010.
Chapter 2 – This is an edited reformatted and augmented version of a Congressional Research Service publication, report RL33646, updated August 2, 2007
Chapter 3 – This is an edited reformatted and augmented version of a Congressional research Service publication, report R41218, May 10, 2010.
Chapter 4 – This is an edited reformatted and augmented version of a Congressional research Service publication, report RL34225, January 21, 2010.
Chapter 5 – This is an edited reformatted and augmented version of a Congressional research Service publication, report RS22737, August 3, 2009.
Chapter 6 – These remarks were delievered as a testimony on September 30, 2009. Senator Richard G. Lugar, East Asian and Pacific Affairs Subcommittee of the Foreign Relations Committee, before the East Asian and Pacific Affairs Subcommittee of the Foreign Relations Committee.
Chapter 7 – These remarks were delivered as a testimony on September 30, 2009. Kurt Campbell, Assistant Secretary of State, Bureau of East Asian and Pacific Affairs, United States Department of State, before the Subcommittee on east Asian and Pcific Affairs Senate Foreign Relations Committee.

Chapter 8 – These remarks were delivered as a testimony on September 30, 2009. Doctor Thant Myint-U, before the East Asia Subcomittee of the Senate Foreign Relations Committee.

Chapter 9 – These remarks were delivered as a testimony on September 30, 2009. David I. Steinberg, Professor, School of Foreign Service, Georgetown University, before the United Senate Subcommittee on Asia and Pacific Affairs

Chapter 10 – These remarks were delivered as a testimony on September 30, 2009. David C. Williams, Executive Director, Center for Constitutional Democracy, John S. Hastings Professor of Law, Indiana University Maurer School of Law, before the Senate Committee on Foreign Relations Subcommittee on East Asia and Pacific Affiars.

INDEX

A

abuse, 48, 58, 60, 96
accommodation, 9
accountability, 17, 111, 120
adaptation, 18
adjustment, 115
advantages, 137
Afghanistan, 15, 33, 48, 83, 86, 121
Africa, 121
agencies, 9, 14, 40
agricultural sector, 42
agriculture, 129, 133
AIDS, 85, 133
Al Qaeda, 13, 39
alien smuggling, 92
annual rate, 7, 22
antithesis, 118
appeasement, 134
appointees, 62, 63
appraisals, 127
appropriations, 93
armed conflict, 115
armed forces, 11, 14, 41, 83, 86, 119, 142, 143
arms trafficking,, 91
arrest, 14, 20, 21, 40, 44, 128
arrests, 10, 15
arsenic, 43
articulation, 131

Asia, vi, vii, viii, ix, 1, 3, 4, 14, 18, 27, 31, 35, 36, 39, 40, 46, 47, 48, 49, 69, 70, 76, 79, 83, 84, 86, 88, 91, 95, 96, 97, 98, 104, 107, 115, 121, 122, 123, 125, 139, 140, 148
assassination, 6, 30, 34, 38
assault, 32
assessment, 34, 66, 80
assets, 62, 70, 73, 100, 102, 103, 130, 135
Association of Southeast Asian Nations (ASEAN), 67, 69, 72, 76, 93, 95, 96, 113, 125, 128, 130, 133, 135
atrocities, 2, 10, 140
Attorney General, 103
autarky, 91
authorities, 14, 18, 40, 41, 80, 81, 92, 98, 110, 111, 112, 123, 133
autonomy, 11, 81

B

background, vii, ix, 27, 99, 108
background information, ix, 27, 99
backlash, 9
ballistic missiles, 91, 110
Bangladesh, v, vii, viii, 1, 2, 3, 4, 5, 6, 7, 8, 9, 10, 11, 12, 13, 14, 15, 16, 17, 18, 19, 20, 21, 22, 23, 24, 25, 26, 27, 28, 29, 30, 31, 32, 33, 34, 35, 36, 37, 38, 39, 40, 41, 42, 43, 44, 45, 46, 47, 48, 49, 84, 98, 115, 135
banking sector, 91

banks, 83, 91, 98, 100, 102, 103, 104
Beijing, 27, 28, 116, 120, 135, 141
Bengal, Bay of, 3, 4, 7, 37, 131
benign, 136
Bhutan, 49
bias, 62
biodiversity, 18, 89
births, 7, 37
black market, 43, 80, 93
blame, 118
blockades, viii, 2, 5, 29
bomb attack, 6, 30, 38
bombing, 15, 34, 42
border control, 93
border security, 10, 45
Britain, 66, 67, 76
budget deficit, 42
buildings, 60
bureaucracy, 82, 117
Bush, George W., ix, 99
business environment, 112

C

Cambodia, 84
campaigns, 118
candidates, 55, 61
Caribbean, 101
censorship, 128
Census, 31
Central Asia, 26, 35, 41, 47
central executive, 63
challenges, 5, 9, 33, 115, 123
child labor, 35, 89
child mortality, 121
China, 2, 4, 18, 19, 20, 21, 28, 35, 43, 46, 49, 67, 69, 76, 82, 84, 90, 93, 95, 96, 104, 105, 107, 113, 118, 119, 120, 129, 131, 132, 133, 134, 141, 145
Christians, 44
CIA, 8, 26, 28, 38, 47, 48
citizenship, 58, 60
City, 47

civil liberties, 55, 58
civil rights, 58
civil servants, 60
civil society, 3, 6, 17, 38, 120, 121, 129
civil war, 6, 37, 115, 119
class, 116
climate, 2, 7, 18, 23, 25, 42
climate change, 2, 7, 18, 23, 25
close relationships, 113
CNN, 97
coal, 22
collusion, viii, 79, 82
color, iv
commander-in-chief, 119
Communist Party, 120, 132
community, 44, 59, 66, 69, 72, 111, 116, 120, 129, 136, 141
community-based organizations, 120
competition, 3
complaints, 11
complexity, 120
compliance, 76, 80, 81
computer software, 128
conditioning, 89
conference, 23
conflict, 5, 9, 33, 85, 116, 120, 140, 142
consensus, 3
consent, 44, 71
conservation, 18
Consolidated Appropriations Act, 68, 71
consolidation, 116
Constitution, v, 51, 56, 75, 112, 142, 143, 144
constitutional amendment, 59
constitutional law, 140
constitutionality, 58
corruption, vii, viii, ix, 1, 2, 5, 29, 31, 32, 33, 34, 38, 44, 48, 79, 80, 82, 83, 90, 95, 101, 103, 112
cost, 24, 56, 62, 107
cotton, 35, 42
counterterrorism, 16, 35
coup, 35, 54

Index

covering, 43
crime, vii, viii, 44, 56, 79, 80, 81, 82, 83, 84, 92, 93, 94, 98, 103
criminal activity, 80, 81
criminal conduct, 105
criminal groups, 82
criticism, 52, 62, 63, 66, 67
cronyism, 35, 82
crops, 43, 84
crude oil, 132
Cuba, 131
cultivation, 83, 86, 87, 94
culture, vii, ix, 9, 79
currency, 83, 90, 92
cyclones, 7, 30, 37, 75, 134

D

deaths, 20, 44, 76, 86
defence, 144
deficit, 42
deforestation, 43
degradation, 24
delegates, 75
delegation, 3, 31, 69
democracy, viii, 2, 3, 16, 17, 20, 30, 32, 35, 51, 52, 53, 54, 56, 66, 68, 71, 72, 75, 92, 95, 110, 111, 115, 117, 123, 127, 128, 131, 139, 140, 141, 144
democratic elections, 37
Democratic Party, 64, 65, 139
democratization, 35, 53, 68
demonstrations, viii, 2, 5, 6, 29, 34, 35, 37, 103
Department of Agriculture, 36
Department of Justice, 92
deposits, 46, 89, 108
destination, 35, 90
destruction, viii, 51, 56, 81, 107
detention, 20, 44, 76, 120, 128
development assistance, 117
diamonds, 95
diet, 24

dignity, 61, 137
diplomacy, 134, 145
disadvantages, 137
disappointment, 66, 70
disaster, 16, 35, 43, 56, 122, 134
disaster relief, 16, 35
displacement, 133
dissatisfaction, 66
dissidents, 120
divergence, 126
diversity, 137
dominance, 42
donors, 35
draft, 12, 54, 56
drinking water, 43
drug trade, 81, 83, 85, 87, 96
drug trafficking, 83, 85, 92
drugs, vii, viii, 79, 80, 82, 85, 87, 88, 90, 93
dynamics, 3, 4, 18, 86, 119, 132

E

earnings, 42, 83, 100
East Asia, v, vi, ix, 69, 70, 88, 96, 105, 107, 109, 115, 139, 147, 148
economic activity, 6, 37, 130
economic assistance, 2
economic development, 35, 100
economic downturn, 22
economic growth, 3, 16, 22, 46, 112
economic integration, 43
economic policy, 136
economic problem, 130
economic reform, 35, 42, 122
economic reforms, 42
economic resources, 23
economy, 14, 24, 30, 31, 38, 41, 42, 80, 93, 107, 115, 117, 118, 120, 122, 132, 133
ecstasy, 88
education, 17, 35, 36
election, 2, 5, 8, 9, 30, 31, 33, 34, 38, 47, 52, 53, 55, 59, 60, 61, 62, 63, 64, 65, 66, 67, 69, 70, 72, 75, 112, 127

electricity, 22
embargo, 72
emergency rule, 30, 31
employees, 63
employment, 131, 132
endangered species, 84
enemies, 116
enforcement, 9, 80, 93, 98
England, 97
environmental effects, 132
environmental issues, 35
environmental protection, 111
equipment, 36
erosion, 23
ethnic groups, 70, 82, 86, 112, 140
ethnic minority, 68, 69, 85, 89, 111, 141
ethnicity, 58
European Union, 62, 76, 93, 112
exaggeration, 132
exclusion, 126
execution, 32
Executive Order, ix, 77, 80, 98, 99, 100, 101, 102, 104
executive orders, 68
exercise, 103, 144
expenditures, 24
experiences, 53
experts, 94, 108
exploitation, 84, 89, 93, 125
exploration, 23, 100
explosives, 14, 15, 33, 41
exporter, 120
export-led growth, 42
exports, 20, 22, 35, 42, 85, 90, 93, 120
exposure, 113, 118, 122, 135
extreme poverty, 115
extremists, vii, 1, 4, 12, 13, 35, 39, 40

F

faith, 144
family members, 10
farmers, 84, 86

fears, 129
fertility, 7, 24
Financial Crimes Enforcement Network, 91, 97
financial records, 60
financial sector, 91
financial support, 62, 102, 112, 121
fish, 8, 37, 98
Fish and Wildlife Service, 96
flooding, 7, 37, 43
fluid, 133
food prices, 24
foreign aid, 131
foreign assistance, 3, 79, 81, 92, 98, 101, 129
foreign banks, 102
foreign investment, 42, 131
foreign policy, 131, 132
France, 8, 27, 28, 38, 47, 48, 49, 76, 96, 98
free trade, 72
freedom, 21, 58, 120, 129
funding, 93, 121

G

general election, 55, 56, 60, 67
Generalized System of Preferences, 101
geography, vii, 1, 23
Germany, 8, 38
gestures, 52, 71
global economy, 93
God, 27
goods and services, 100
governance, vii, viii, 1, 3, 29, 39, 112, 118, 122, 126, 127, 130, 136, 137
green revolution, 24
growth rate, 7, 24, 37

H

harassment, 20, 55
hardwoods, 93
hegemony, 12
heroin, 85, 86, 87, 133

Index

HIV, 85, 121, 133
HIV/AIDS, 133
Hong Kong, 35, 97
hostilities, 82, 119
housing, 60
hub, 14, 40
human capital, 130
human rights, vii, ix, 2, 3, 5, 16, 17, 20, 21, 30, 33, 35, 44, 52, 68, 75, 79, 86, 92, 101, 110, 111, 126, 129, 131, 132, 135, 145
humanitarian aid, 95, 129, 141
hurricanes, 75
hydroelectric power, 43, 120

I

ice, 24, 28
idealism, 136
ideology, 4, 60
illiteracy, 9, 32
image, 44, 45
immigrants, 45, 133
immunity, 80
impacts, 23
import ban, 100
import restrictions, 72, 77
imports, 24, 79
inclusion, 38, 102
independence, vii, viii, 1, 2, 6, 9, 10, 19, 29, 35, 36, 37
Independence, 142
India, vii, viii, 1, 2, 4, 6, 9, 10, 13, 14, 15, 18, 19, 20, 24, 25, 27, 28, 29, 35, 36, 39, 40, 41, 42, 43, 45, 46, 47, 48, 49, 69, 76, 82, 84, 95, 98, 107, 113, 120, 131, 132, 133, 134
Indonesia, 67, 76, 84, 130, 135
inefficiency, 42
inflation, 112
inheritance, 12
initiation, 111
insecurity, 86
insight, 113

insurgency, 11, 90, 116, 144
integration, 43
intellectual property, 3
intelligence, 14, 16, 40, 41, 45, 70, 91, 102, 132
interference, 82, 143, 144
international financial institutions, 71, 92, 100
International Financial Institutions, 117, 122
international terrorism, 20
intervention, vii, viii, 1, 6, 29, 141
intimidation, 35, 56
investors, 102, 103
Iran, 108
Iraq, 35
Islam, 9, 13, 21, 32, 40, 44
Islamic state, 16
Islamic world, 2, 16, 30, 35
Islamism, 27
Islamist extremists, vii, 1, 35
isolation, 93, 116, 117, 122, 123
Israel, 44
issues, 17, 34, 43, 45, 52, 68, 72, 80, 81, 92, 108, 111, 116, 122, 126, 128, 133, 134, 135, 140

J

Jamestown, 47
Japan, 35, 43, 67, 76, 91, 93, 105, 107, 113, 132
Jews, 44
journalists, 10, 20, 44
judicial branch, 57, 58
judiciary, 5, 33
jurisdiction, 103, 104
justification, 132

K

Korea, 76, 84, 91, 97, 104, 105, 107, 108, 109, 110, 130, 131, 132, 133
Kuwait, 16, 35

Index

L

labeling, 140
labor force, 42
landscape, 2, 4, 8, 9, 30, 32, 118
Laos, 84, 96, 98, 129
law enforcement, 9, 80, 93, 98
leadership, 11, 12, 15, 57, 60, 63, 69, 87, 110, 111, 112, 113, 117, 119, 120, 122, 136, 142
legislation, 45, 57, 58, 73, 128, 134
lending, 43
livestock, 43
living conditions, 120
local government, 123
lying, vii, 1, 7, 18, 23, 37

M

magazines, 120
majority, vii, viii, 1, 2, 5, 29, 62, 104
malaria, 121, 133
Malaysia, 82, 84, 107
management, 18, 43
manufacturing, 42, 87
Margesson, Rhoda, 75
maritime security, 16
market access, 22, 131
market economy, 43, 117
market share, 131
media, 17, 39, 45, 86, 88, 89, 90, 112, 120
membership, 58, 60, 63
memory, 110
messages, 69
meter, 25
methamphetamine, 84, 85, 87
Middle East, 19, 35, 47, 120
migrants, 89, 107
migration, 45, 119, 130, 133
militancy, vii, viii, 1, 14, 29, 40, 44
military, vii, viii, 1, 2, 4, 5, 6, 7, 8, 10, 11, 16, 29, 30, 31, 32, 35, 37, 51, 53, 54, 57, 58, 59, 63, 65, 67, 70, 71, 72, 75, 79, 80, 82, 83, 85, 89, 90, 91, 93, 110, 112, 113, 116, 118, 122, 123, 126, 127, 128, 129, 130, 132, 133, 135, 136, 137, 140, 141, 142, 143, 144, 145
military dictatorship, 118, 144
military government, 54, 71, 129
military junta, viii, 51, 53, 54, 59, 67, 72, 75, 79, 80
militia, 82, 119, 144
mining, 80, 89, 90
minorities, 44, 68, 69, 71, 107, 111, 113, 128, 130, 134, 137, 140, 141
minority groups, 21, 34, 69, 85, 89, 111
minors, 89
modification, 126
momentum, 111, 117
money laundering, 82, 83, 91, 92, 97, 103, 104, 133
Mongolia, 105
morale, 11
morbidity, 121
mortality rate, 121
murder, 13, 40
music, 120
Muslims, 6, 44
Myanmar, vii, viii, 53, 57, 64, 65, 66, 67, 74, 75, 76, 77, 79, 87, 91, 95, 96, 97, 98, 102, 104, 125, 126, 128, 129, 131, 132, 133, 134, 135, 136, 137

N

narcotics, 83, 84, 85, 91, 92, 93, 98, 111, 133, 134
national interests, 132, 136
National Party, viii, 2, 4, 5, 6, 8, 13, 14, 29, 30, 31, 33, 37, 39, 40, 64, 65
national security, 19, 95, 132
nationalism, 12
nationalists, 10
natural disasters, 11, 23
natural gas, 3, 22, 30, 46, 93, 100, 102, 103, 120, 131

natural resource management, 18
natural resources, 26, 89, 122
needy, 121, 122
negotiating, 134
Nepal, 14, 41, 43, 49
New York, iv
NGOs, 49, 112, 130, 135
nodes, 89
North Korea, 91, 97, 104, 105, 107, 108, 109, 110, 132, 133
Norway, 76
nuclear program, 108
nuclear weapons, 91
nutrition, 129, 133

O

Obama Administration, 52, 53, 68, 69, 73, 107
Obama, President, 52, 69, 70, 73
obstacles, 39, 123
oil, 120, 132
oligopoly, 32
Omnibus Appropriations Act,, 77
openness, 113
opportunities, 71, 113, 116, 117, 123, 126, 127
opposition parties, 3, 8, 31, 55, 62, 65, 69, 127
organizing, 86
overlap, 134
oversight, 9, 80, 81, 91, 116
ownership, 98, 100

P

Pacific, v, vi, ix, 16, 27, 69, 75, 96, 97, 105, 107, 109, 125, 139, 147, 148
Pakistan, vii, viii, 1, 2, 6, 9, 10, 14, 15, 16, 18, 19, 27, 29, 36, 41, 42, 45, 48, 49, 115
paradigm, 24
parallel, 111
parity, 42
partition, 6

peacekeeping, 2, 11, 16, 31, 35
penalties, 89, 102
per capita income, 42
performance, 8, 135
permission, iv, 128
permit, 144
pessimism, 34
Philippines, 76
photographs, 32
pipelines, 132
piracy, 39
plants, 108
pluralism, 129
police, 4, 12, 15, 33, 39, 82, 95
policy makers, 95
policy options, 107
political affiliations, 4
political leaders, 9, 52, 57, 113, 142
political meeting, 32
political opposition, 6, 38, 120
political participation, 66
political parties, viii, 4, 9, 12, 30, 31, 33, 34, 42, 51, 52, 59, 60, 62, 63, 67, 68, 129
political party, 10, 60, 61, 62, 63, 66, 128
politics, viii, 2, 6, 11, 13, 29, 32, 37, 40, 66, 118, 126
population density, 25
population growth, 3, 24
portfolio, 142
ports, 18, 19
positive relationship, 110
poverty, vii, viii, 1, 5, 7, 9, 29, 33, 84, 115, 118, 122, 129
poverty line, 7, 84, 129
poverty reduction, 122
prisoners, 66, 67, 68, 70, 71, 111, 112, 120, 128
private banks, 91
privatization, 42
producers, 85, 87
profit, 112, 116
programming, 98
project, 100, 102, 103

proliferation, 36, 107, 108, 110
protectionism, 43
public sector, 42, 130
public welfare, 58
public-private partnerships, 22
punishment, 118
purchasing power, 42
purchasing power parity, 42

Q

qualifications, 61, 143

R

radicals, 7, 32, 38
rape, 140
reactions, 134
reading, 140, 142
reality, 127, 128, 136, 140, 141, 144
recall, 143
reception, 59
recognition, 131
recommendations, iv, 33, 141, 144
reconciliation, 66, 67, 68, 116
reconstruction, 83
reforms, 2, 29, 31, 42, 72, 112, 117, 136
refugees, 21, 25, 89, 107, 141
relatives, 92
relaxation, 128
relief, 88, 128
religion, 21, 58, 60
remittances, 42, 92, 100
reparation, 134
reporters, 66
repression, 117, 120
reputation, vii, 1, 5, 11, 61
requirements, 46, 58, 103, 136
reserves, 3, 4, 22, 23, 30, 42, 46, 68
resettlement, 107
resilience, 2, 23
resistance, 42, 80, 140, 141
resistance groups, 140, 142
resolution, 10, 72, 77

resource management, 18
resources, 16, 19, 23, 25, 46, 47, 90, 100, 101, 122
respect, 52, 68, 137, 141
restructuring, 71
retaliation, 11
retirement, 62, 117
revenue, 22, 93, 95
rhino, 98
rights, iv, vii, ix, 2, 3, 5, 12, 16, 17, 20, 21, 30, 33, 35, 44, 45, 52, 58, 68, 75, 79, 86, 92, 101, 110, 111, 126, 129, 131, 132, 135, 145
river systems, 7, 37
rockets, 91
rubber, 97
rule of law, vii, ix, 3, 79, 80, 112, 135
rural areas, 84
Russia, 76, 108

S

safe haven, 95
safe havens, 95
salinity, 23, 43
sanctions, ix, 52, 53, 68, 70, 71, 72, 73, 76, 77, 79, 80, 81, 83, 90, 91, 92, 93, 95, 98, 99, 101, 103, 107, 109, 111, 112, 117, 118, 122, 123, 125, 127, 129, 130, 131, 133, 134, 136, 139, 145
sanctuaries, 131
Saudi Arabia, 16
scaling, 121
sea level, 23, 25, 37
seafood, 8, 37, 89
Secretary of the Treasury, 70, 71, 83, 91, 103, 104
security forces, 9, 45
self-expression, 6
seminars, 52
Senate, vi, ix, 27, 71, 73, 80, 81, 98, 105, 115, 125, 139, 147, 148

Index

Senate Foreign Relations Committee, vi, ix, 105, 115, 147, 148
sex, 89
shape, 109
Sharia, 13, 32, 39, 40
sheep, 66
shock, 44
shortage, 86
shrimp, 97
signs, 31, 52, 65, 69, 70
Singapore, 35, 67, 69, 76, 83, 96, 104, 105, 107
slaves, 84
smuggling, 82, 88, 89, 90, 92
Smuggling, 96
social change, 118, 130
software, 128
solidarity, 142, 144
Somalia, 83
South Asia, vii, 1, 3, 14, 18, 19, 35, 39, 40, 42, 43, 47, 48, 49
South China Sea, 132
South Korea, 76, 84, 107, 130, 131
Southeast Asia, vii, viii, 14, 36, 40, 46, 67, 76, 79, 84, 86, 93, 95, 96, 97, 121, 139, 140
sovereignty, 142
space, 12, 13, 30, 39, 127
specialists, 125
species, 84
speculation, 91
speech, 75
Sri Lanka, 19, 49
stakeholders, 110, 112
State Department, 6, 13, 16, 17, 21, 35, 38, 39, 41, 53, 66, 69, 76, 81, 82, 83, 84, 87, 89, 91, 92, 93, 98, 102, 141
state of emergency, 5, 21, 32, 58, 144
statistics, 48, 140
statutes, 143
stimulus, 22
storage, 43
storms, 75
strategy, 11, 19, 85, 123, 144
structuring, 20
substitutes, 86
Sudan, 121
sugarcane, 97
Suharto, 135
suicide, 34
suppression, 55, 81, 103
Supreme Court, 58, 63
survival, 141
suspects, 44
Syria, 108

T

tactics, 5, 126, 134, 136
Taiwan, 98, 131
Taliban, 14, 34, 41
tariff, 39, 101
tax evasion, 32
technical assistance, 33, 71, 128
temperature, 23
tension, 85
tensions, 11, 20, 25, 81, 126
tenure, 6, 37
territory, 20, 75, 104
terrorism, 12, 14, 15, 20, 36, 40, 41, 42, 92, 135
terrorist groups, 13, 14, 40, 41
terrorist organization, 13, 39
terrorists, 95, 103
textiles, 42
Thailand, 76, 82, 84, 85, 87, 89, 90, 95, 96, 98, 100, 104, 107, 116, 120, 129, 130
thoughts, 44
threats, 91, 126
Title I, 36, 71, 95, 105
Title II, 36, 71, 105
torture, 44
tourism, 117, 118, 135
trade agreement, 72
trading partner, 3
trafficking in persons, 44, 81, 88, 92

training, 14, 15, 40, 41, 42, 98, 108, 117, 119, 123, 130, 135
tranches, 131
transactions, 73, 92, 98, 100, 103, 104
translation, 75, 76
transparency, 17, 92, 108, 136
transport, viii, 2, 5, 29, 120
transportation, 19, 83, 101
Treasury Department, 100, 101, 104
treaties, 57, 85
trial, 71, 98, 128
tropical storms, 75
tuberculosis, 133
turnout, 56

U

U.N. Security Council, 67, 72, 97
U.S. Department of the Treasury, 96, 105
U.S. policy, 2, 16, 30, 68, 79, 80, 81, 95, 107, 109, 110, 129, 133, 136
U.S. Treasury, 62, 92
uniform, 11, 66
United Kingdom (UK), 33, 47, 117
United Nations (UN), 4, 11, 21, 26, 28, 33, 76, 83, 85, 86, 88, 96, 107, 109, 117, 121, 122, 126, 128, 130, 140, 145
United Nations High Commissioner for Refugees (UNHCR), 21, 107
universities, 117
uranium, 95, 108
urban population, 7, 24
urbanization, 7, 24
USDA, 36, 73, 76

V

variations, 75

vehicles, 60, 95
veto, 59, 128
victims, 84, 93, 112
Vietnam, 76, 84, 105, 129, 139, 140
violence, vii, viii, 1, 2, 4, 5, 6, 8, 10, 20, 21, 29, 30, 34, 35, 38, 44, 95, 130, 133, 141, 144
visa, 76
vision, 111
voters, 34, 53, 56, 61
voting, 31, 56, 60, 128
vulnerability, 16

W

waiver, 73
war crimes, 2, 9, 10, 72
War on Terror, 27, 48
watershed, 115, 118, 120
wealth, 42
weapons, 85, 90, 91, 107, 109
weapons of mass destruction, 107
welfare, 58
wildlife, vii, viii, 79, 80, 84, 90, 93, 98, 134
withdrawal, 11, 120
witnesses, 108
WMD, 110
workers, 22, 24, 120, 121, 130
working conditions, 35, 131
World Bank, 8, 38, 49, 122, 129, 136
World War I, 54, 111, 134
worry, 142

Z

Zimbabwe, 121